Mathematics:

Worded Problems

Book 1

How to use this book to make the most of 11 plus exam preparation

It is important to remember that for 11 plus exams there is no national syllabus, no pass mark and no retake option. It is therefore vital that your child is fully primed to perform to the best of their ability so that they give themselves the best possible chance on the day.

Mathematics: Worded Problems

This topic-based workbook has been designed to consolidate core 11 plus mathematics knowledge through a series of graded questions: Beginner, Intermediate and Advanced. Each chapter covers a different mathematics topic and comprises 15 questions at each of the difficulty levels. The questions are typical of the mathematics and numerical reasoning sections of the 11 plus and Common Entrance exams. The questioned have been designed to be answered without the use of a calculator. Additional paper should be used for any rough working out.

Never has it been more useful to learn from mistakes!

Students can improve by as much as 15%, not only by focused practice, but also by targeting any weak areas.

How to manage your child's practice

To get the most up-to-date information, visit our website, www.elevenplusexams.co.uk, the UK's largest online resource for 11 plus, with over 65,000 webpages and a forum administered by a select group of experienced moderators.

About the authors

The Eleven Plus Exams' **First Past The Post®** series has been created by a team of experienced tutors and authors from leading British universities.

Published by Technical One Ltd t/a Eleven Plus Exams

With special thanks to all the children who tested our material at the ElevenPlusExams centre in Harrow.

ISBN: 978-1-912364-45-9 (previously 978-1-908684-80-6)

Copyright © ElevenPlusExams.co.uk 2018

Second edition

About Us

At Eleven Plus Exams, we supply high-quality 11 plus tuition for your children. Our free website at **www.elevenplusexams.co.uk** is the largest website in the UK that specifically prepares children for the 11 plus exams. We also provide online services to schools and our **First Past The Post®** range of books has been well-received by schools, tuition centres and parents.

Eleven Plus Exams is recognised as a trusted and authoritative source. We have been quoted in numerous national newspapers, including *The Telegraph*, *The Observer*, the *Daily Mail* and *The Sunday Telegraph*, as well as on national television (BBC1 and Channel 4), and BBC radio.

Our website offers a vast amount of information and advice on the 11 plus, including a moderated online forum, books, downloadable material and online services to enhance your child's chances of success. Set up in 2004, the website grew from an initial 20 webpages to more than 65,000 today, and has been visited by millions of parents. It is moderated by experts in the field, who provide support for parents both before and after the exams.

Don't forget to visit **www.elevenplusexams.co.uk** and see why we are the market's leading one-stop shop for all your 11 plus needs. You will find:

- ✓ Comprehensive quality content and advice written by 11 plus experts

- ✓ Eleven Plus Exams online shop supplying a wide range of practice books, e-papers, software and apps

- ✓ Lots of FREE practice papers to download

- ✓ Professional tuition service

- ✓ Short revision courses

- ✓ Year-long 11 plus courses

- ✓ Mock exams tailored to reflect those of the main examining bodies

978-1-912364-60-2	Verbal Reasoning: Cloze Tests Book 1 - Mixed Format
978-1-912364-61-9	Verbal Reasoning: Cloze Tests Book 2 - Mixed Format
978-1-912364-78-7	Verbal Reasoning: Cloze Tests Book 3 - Mixed Format
978-1-912364-79-4	Verbal Reasoning: Cloze Tests Book 4 - Mixed Format
978-1-912364-62-6	Verbal Reasoning: Vocabulary Book 1 - Multiple Choice
978-1-912364-63-3	Verbal Reasoning: Vocabulary Book 2 - Multiple Choice
978-1-912364-64-0	Verbal Reasoning: Vocabulary Book 3 - Multiple Choice
978-1-912364-65-7	Verbal Reasoning: Vocabulary, Spelling and Grammar Book 1 - Multiple Choice
978-1-912364-66-4	Verbal Reasoning: Vocabulary, Spelling and Grammar Book 2 - Multiple Choice
978-1-912364-68-8	Verbal Reasoning: Vocabulary in Context Level 1
978-1-912364-69-5	Verbal Reasoning: Vocabulary in Context Level 2
978-1-912364-70-1	Verbal Reasoning: Vocabulary in Context Level 3
978-1-912364-71-8	Verbal Reasoning: Vocabulary in Context Level 4
978-1-912364-74-9	Verbal Reasoning: Vocabulary Puzzles Book 1
978-1-912364-75-6	Verbal Reasoning: Vocabulary Puzzles Book 2
978-1-912364-76-3	Verbal Reasoning: Practice Papers Book 1 - Multiple Choice
978-1-912364-77-0	Verbal Reasoning: Practice Papers Book 2 - Multiple Choice

978-1-912364-02-2	English: Comprehensions Classic Literature Book 1 - Multiple Choice
978-1-912364-03-9	English: Comprehensions Classic Literature Book 2 - Multiple Choice
978-1-912364-05-3	English: Comprehensions Contemporary Literature Book 1 - Multiple Choice
978-1-912364-06-0	English: Comprehensions Contemporary Literature Book 2 - Multiple Choice
978-1-912364-08-4	English: Comprehensions Non-Fiction Book 1 - Multiple Choice
978-1-912364-09-1	English: Comprehensions Non-Fiction Book 2 - Multiple Choice
978-1-912364-23-7	English: Comprehensions Poetry Book 1 - Multiple Choice
978-1-912364-14-5	English: Mini Comprehensions - Inference Book 1
978-1-912364-15-2	English: Mini Comprehensions - Inference Book 2
978-1-912364-16-9	English: Mini Comprehensions - Inference Book 3
978-1-912364-11-4	English: Mini Comprehensions - Fact-Finding Book 1
978-1-912364-12-1	English: Mini Comprehensions - Fact-Finding Book 2
978-1-912364-21-3	English: Spelling, Punctuation and Grammar Book 1
978-1-912364-22-0	English: Spelling, Punctuation and Grammar Book 2
978-1-912364-00-8	English: Practice Papers Book 1 - Multiple Choice
978-1-912364-01-5	English: Practice Papers Book 2 - Multiple Choice
978-1-912364-17-6	Creative Writing Examples

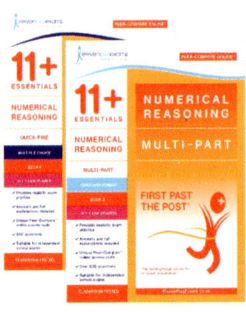

978-1-912364-30-5	Numerical Reasoning: Quick-Fire Book 1
978-1-912364-31-2	Numerical Reasoning: Quick-Fire Book 2
978-1-912364-32-9	Numerical Reasoning: Quick-Fire Book 1 - Multiple Choice
978-1-912364-33-6	Numerical Reasoning: Quick-Fire Book 2 - Multiple Choice
978-1-912364-34-3	Numerical Reasoning: Multi-Part Book 1
978-1-912364-35-0	Numerical Reasoning: Multi-Part Book 2
978-1-912364-36-7	Numerical Reasoning: Multi-Part Book 1 - Multiple Choice
978-1-912364-37-4	Numerical Reasoning: Multi-Part Book 2 - Multiple Choice

978-1-912364-43-5	Mathematics: Mental Arithmetic Book 1
978-1-912364-44-2	Mathematics: Mental Arithmetic Book 2
978-1-912364-45-9	Mathematics: Worded Problems Book 1
978-1-912364-46-6	Mathematics: Worded Problems Book 2
978-1-912364-52-7	Mathematics: Worded Problems Book 3
978-1-912364-47-3	Mathematics: Dictionary Plus
978-1-912364-50-3	Mathematics: Crossword Puzzles Book 1
978-1-912364-51-0	Mathematics: Crossword Puzzles Book 2
978-1-912364-48-0	Mathematics: Practice Papers Book 1 - Multiple Choice
978-1-912364-49-7	Mathematics: Practice Papers Book 2 - Multiple Choice

978-1-912364-87-9	Non-Verbal Reasoning: 2D Book 1 - Multiple Choice
978-1-912364-88-6	Non-Verbal Reasoning: 2D Book 2 - Multiple Choice
978-1-912364-85-5	Non-Verbal Reasoning: 3D Book 1 - Multiple Choice
978-1-912364-86-2	Non-Verbal Reasoning: 3D Book 2 - Multiple Choice
978-1-912364-83-1	Non-Verbal Reasoning: Practice Papers Book 1 - Multiple Choice

Contents

This workbook comprises 14 chapters, each covering a different topic at three different levels of difficulty: Beginner, Intermediate and Advanced. Each chapter comprises 45 questions.

Glossary

Learn the meanings of the terms listed below to expand your mathematical vocabulary.

Apothem - a line segment from the centre of a regular polygon to the midpoint of one of its sides.

Bearing - an angle given in three figures that is measured clockwise from the north direction, e.g. 025°.

BIDMAS - an acronym for **B**rackets, **I**ndices, **D**ivision and **M**ultiplication, and **A**ddition and **S**ubtraction. It is the agreed order of operations used to clarify which should be performed first in a given expression.

Bimodal - when a collection of data has two modes, e.g. in the dataset: {1, 1, 1, 2, 4, 5, 5, 5}, the two modes are 1 and 5.

Bisect - to divide into two equal parts.

Coefficient - a constant that is placed before a variable in an algebraic expression, e.g. in the term $4x$, the coefficient is 4.

Complementary angles - two angles are complementary if they add up to 90°.

Cube number - a number that can be produced by multiplying another number by itself twice, e.g. 8 (= 2 × 2 × 2).

Edge - a line segment that joins two vertices of a 2D shape, or a line segment at which two faces meet in a 3D shape.

Enlargement - a type of transformation in which the size of an object is changed, whilst the ratio of the lengths of its sides stays the same.

Equidistant - two or more points are equidistant if they are the same distance from a common point.

Face - an individual surface of a 3D shape.

Fair - free from bias or equally likely to occur.

Gallon - a unit of volume used for measuring liquids. It is equal to 8 pints, or 4.55 litres.

Gradient - a measure of the steepness of a straight line.

Highest common factor (HCF) - the largest number that is a factor of two or more given numbers, e.g. 5 is the highest common factor of 10 and 15.

Imperial units - the system of units first defined in the British Weights and Measures Act. These units are no longer officially used in Britain, e.g. inches, feet, pints etc.

Inscribe - to draw a shape within another so that their edges touch, but do not intersect.

Integer - a whole number, i.e. not a decimal or a fraction.

Isosceles trapezium - a trapezium with one line of symmetry, two pairs of equal angles and one pair of parallel sides.

Leap year - a calendar year that occurs every four years. It has 366 days, instead of 365, and includes the 29th February. The year 2012 was a leap year.

Lowest common multiple (LCM) - the smallest number that is a multiple of two or more given numbers, e.g. 6 is the lowest common multiple of 2 and 3.

Metric units - a system of units based on multiples of 10, e.g. millimetre (mm), centimetre (cm) or metre (m).

Net - a 2D pattern that can be cut out and folded to make a 3D shape.

Parallel - lines that run side-by-side, always remain the same distance apart and never intersect, even if they are extended.

Perimeter - the total distance around the outside of a 2D shape.

Perpendicular - two lines are perpendicular if they are at an angle of 90° to each other.

Polygon - a 2D shape with three or more straight sides and no curved sides, e.g. triangle, pentagon, hexagon.

Polyhedron - a 3D shape whose faces are polygons, e.g. triangular pyramid, octahedron.

Prime factor - one of a collection of prime numbers whose product is a particular number, i.e. 2 × 2 × 3 = 12, so 2, 2 and 3 are the prime factors of 12.

Prime number - an integer greater than 1 that has no factors other than 1 and itself, e.g. 2, 3, 5.

Prism - a solid 3D shape with two identical, parallel end faces that are connected by flat sides.

Pyramid - a solid 3D shape whose base is a polygon and has triangular faces that meet at a single vertex.

Quadrilateral - a 2D shape with four straight sides. Quadrilaterals are polygons.

Reflective symmetry - a shape or an object has reflective symmetry if an imaginary line can be drawn that divides the shape into two, so that one half is a reflection of the other in the imaginary line.

Regular - a regular polygon has sides of equal length.

Remainder - a number that is left over after a division.

Rotational symmetry - a shape or an object has rotational symmetry if it can be rotated, but still appears to be in the same original position, e.g. a square has rotational symmetry of four, because it can be rotated four times, but still appears the same.

Scalene - the sides of a scalene triangle are all of different lengths.

Sequence - a list of numbers or objects arranged in a particular order, which is defined by a specific rule, or set of rules.

Square number - a number that can be produced by multiplying another number by itself, e.g. 16 (= 4 × 4).

Supplementary angles - two angles are supplementary if they add up to 180°.

Triangle - a 2D shape with three straight sides. Triangles are polygons.

Triangular number - a number that can be represented by a group of equally spaced points arranged in a triangle, e.g. 1, 3, 6: • ⁛ ⁘

Vertex - a point at which two or more straight lines meet.

Place Value

The numerical value of a digit in a number.

For example, in the number 1234.567, the digit 3 has a place value of tens.

1	2	3	4	.	5	6	7
thousands	hundreds	tens	units	decimal point	tenths	hundredths	thousandths

Special Numbers

	1st	2nd	3rd	4th	5th	6th	7th	8th	9th	10th	11th	12th	13th	14th	15th	16th	17th	18th	19th	20th
even	2	4	6	8	10	12	14	16	18	20	22	24	26	28	30	32	34	36	38	40
odd	1	3	5	7	9	11	13	15	17	19	21	23	25	27	29	31	33	35	37	39
square	1	4	9	16	25	36	49	64	81	100	121	144	169	196	225	256	289	324	361	400
cube	1	8	27	64	125	216	343	512	729	1000	1331	1728	2197	2744	3375	4096	4913	5832	6859	8000
triangular	1	3	6	10	15	21	28	36	45	55	66	78	91	105	120	136	153	171	190	210
prime	2	3	5	7	11	13	17	19	23	29	31	37	41	43	47	53	59	61	67	71
fibonacci	1	1	2	3	5	8	13	21	34	55	89	144	233	377	610	987	1597	2584	4181	6765

Equivalent Decimals, Fractions & Percentages

percentage	5%	10%	15%	20%	25%	30%	35%	40%	45%	50%	55%	60%	65%	70%	75%	80%	85%	90%	95%	100%	150%
fraction	$\frac{1}{20}$	$\frac{1}{10}$	$\frac{3}{20}$	$\frac{1}{5}$	$\frac{1}{4}$	$\frac{3}{10}$	$\frac{7}{20}$	$\frac{2}{5}$	$\frac{9}{20}$	$\frac{1}{2}$	$\frac{11}{20}$	$\frac{3}{5}$	$\frac{13}{20}$	$\frac{7}{10}$	$\frac{3}{4}$	$\frac{4}{5}$	$\frac{17}{20}$	$\frac{9}{10}$	$\frac{19}{20}$	$\frac{1}{1}$	$\frac{3}{2}$
decimal	0.05	0.1	0.15	0.2	0.25	0.3	0.35	0.4	0.45	0.5	0.55	0.6	0.65	0.7	0.75	0.8	0.85	0.9	0.95	1	1.5

Mathematical Symbols

+	addition
−	subtraction
×	multiplication
÷	division
±	positive or negative
=	equals sign
<	less than
>	greater than
≈	approximately equal to
≤	less than or equal to
≥	greater than or equal to
≠	not equal to
a^2	squared number
a^3	cubed number
%	per cent
$\sqrt{a}$	square root
$\sqrt[3]{a}$	cubed root
$\dot{a}$	recurring number
$a{:}b$	ratio
$a°$	degrees
$\bar{a}$	mean
(x, y)	coordinates
⌐	right angle
$\binom{x}{y}$	column vector (column matrix)
a/b	fraction
$\{a, b\}$	dataset
π	pi

Equivalent Periods of Time

1 minute	60 seconds
1 hour	60 minutes
1 day	24 hours
1 week	7 days
1 year	12 months (365 days)
1 leap year	366 days
1 decade	10 years
1 century	100 years
1 millennium	1,000 years

Roman Numerals

When a symbol appears *after* a numerically larger symbol, their values are added. When a symbol appears *before* a numerically larger symbol, their values are subtracted.

1	I		40	XL
2	II		50	L
3	III		60	LX
4	IV		70	LXX
5	V		80	LXXX
6	VI		90	XC
7	VII		100	C
8	VIII		200	CC
9	IX		300	CCC
10	X		400	CD
20	XX		500	D
30	XXX		1,000	M

Time Conversion

24-hour clock	12-hour clock
00:00	12.00am
01:00	1.00am
02:00	2.00am
03:00	3.00am
04:00	4.00am
05:00	5.00am
06:00	6.00am
07:00	7.00am
08:00	8.00am
09:00	9.00am
10:00	10.00am
11:00	11.00am
12:00	12.00pm
13:00	1.00pm
14:00	2.00pm
15:00	3.00pm
16:00	4.00pm
17:00	5.00pm
18:00	6.00pm
19:00	7.00pm
20:00	8.00pm
21:00	9.00pm
22:00	10.00pm
23:00	11.00pm

Units of Measurement

	Metric system		Imperial system		
	Units	Conversion	Units	Conversion	Metric approximation
Mass	milligram (mg)	1mg = 0.1cg = 0.001g	ounce (oz)	1oz = $\frac{1}{16}$ lb	1oz ≈ 28g
	centigram (cg)	1cg = 10mg = 0.01g	pound (lb)	1lb = 16oz	1lb ≈ 0.45kg
	gram (g)	1g = 100cg = 0.001kg	stone (st)	1st = 14lb	1st ≈ 6kg
	kilogram (kg)	1kg = 1,000g = 0.001t			
	tonne (t)	1t = 1,000,000g = 1,000kg	ton	1 ton = 160st	1 ton ≈ 0.91 tonne
Length	millimetre (mm)	1mm = 0.1cm = 0.001m	inch (in or ")	1in = $\frac{1}{12}$ ft	1in ≈ 25mm
	centimetre (cm)	1cm = 10mm = 0.01m	foot (ft or ')	1ft = 12in	1ft ≈ 30cm
	metre (m)	1m = 100cm = 0.001km	yard (yd)	1yd = 3ft	1yd ≈ 91cm
	kilometre (km)	1km = 100,000cm = 1,000m	mile	1 mile = 1,760yd	1 mile ≈ 1.6km
Volume	millilitre (ml)	1ml = 0.1cl = 0.001l = 1cm^3	fluid ounce (fl. oz)	1fl. oz = $\frac{1}{20}$ pt	1fl. oz ≈ 28ml
	centilitre (cl)	1cl = 10ml = 0.01l = 10cm^3	pint (pt)	1pt = 20fl. oz	1pt ≈ 0.57l
	litre (l)	1l = 100cl = 0.001kl = 1,000cm^3			
	kilolitre (kl)	1kl = 1,000l = 1,000,000cm^3	gallon (gal)	1gal = 8pt	1gal ≈ 4.5l

Types of Angles

Zero angle
Equivalent to 0°

The angle AÔB is an example of a zero angle.

Acute angle
An angle greater than 0°, but smaller than 90°

Angle $c°$ (AÔB) is an example of an acute angle.

Right angle
An angle of 90°

Angle $d°$ (AÔB) is an example of a right angle.

Obtuse angle
An angle greater than 90°, but smaller than 180°

Angle $e°$ (AÔB) is an example of an obtuse angle.

Flat angle
An angle of 180°

The angle AÔB is an example of a flat angle.

Reflex angle
An angle greater than 180°, but smaller than 360°

Angle $f°$ (AÔB) is an example of a reflex angle.

Full rotation
A full turn, equal to 360°

Pairs of Angles

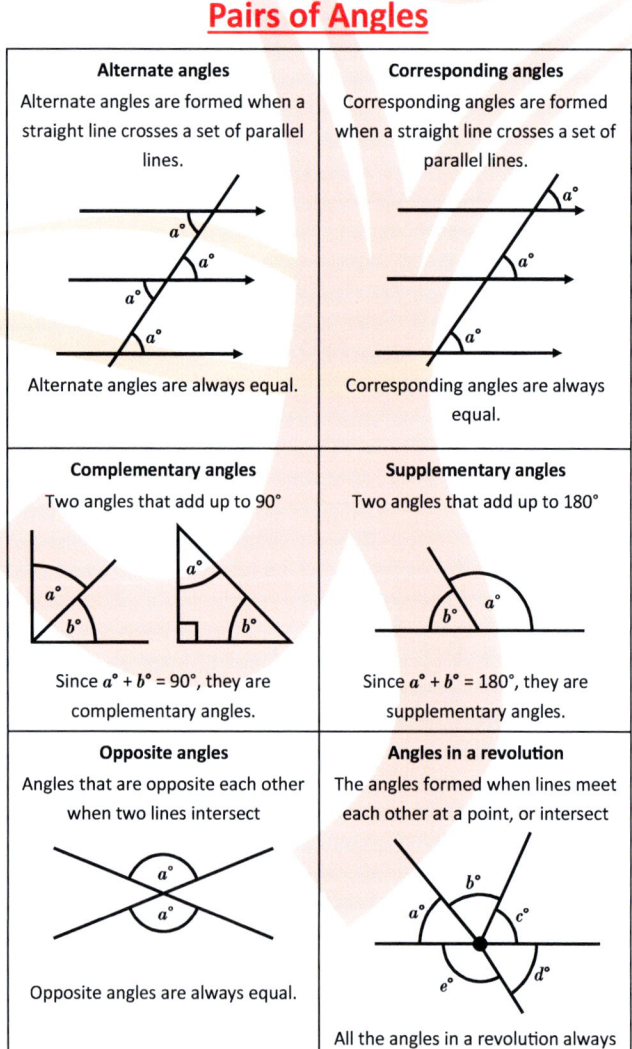

Alternate angles
Alternate angles are formed when a straight line crosses a set of parallel lines.

Alternate angles are always equal.

Corresponding angles
Corresponding angles are formed when a straight line crosses a set of parallel lines.

Corresponding angles are always equal.

Complementary angles
Two angles that add up to 90°

Since $a° + b° = 90°$, they are complementary angles.

Supplementary angles
Two angles that add up to 180°

Since $a° + b° = 180°$, they are supplementary angles.

Opposite angles
Angles that are opposite each other when two lines intersect

Opposite angles are always equal.

Angles in a revolution
The angles formed when lines meet each other at a point, or intersect

All the angles in a revolution always add up to 360°. Here, $a° + b° + c° + d° + e° = 360°$.

2D Shapes

Figures with two dimensions: length and width.

Circle	Right-angled triangle	Equilateral triangle	Isosceles triangle	Scalene triangle
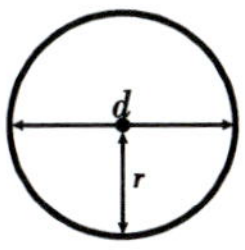 r = radius d = diameter The perimeter of a circle is its circumference.	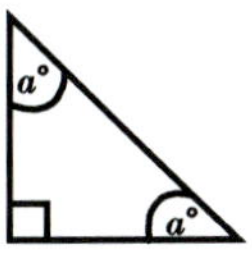 One angle is a right angle (90°). The other two angles are complementary.	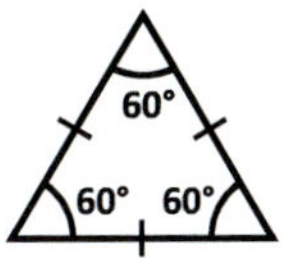 All three angles are equal (60°). All three sides are of equal length.	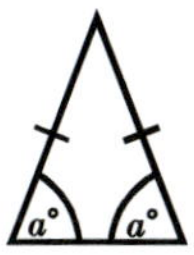 Two angles are equal. Two sides are of equal length.	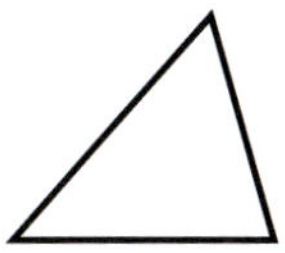 No angles are equal. No sides are of equal length.
Square	**Trapezium**	**Rhombus**	**Parallelogram**	**Kite**
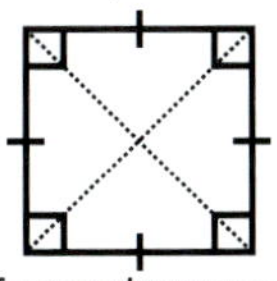 All four angles are equal (90°). All four sides are of equal length. The diagonals bisect each other at 90°.	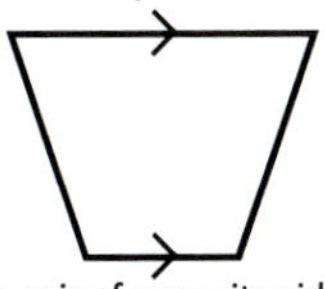 One pair of opposite sides is parallel.	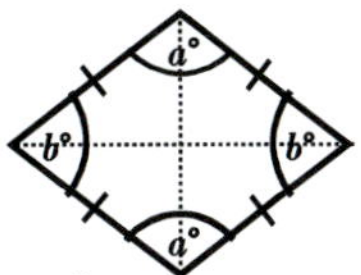 Opposite angles are equal. All sides are of equal length. The diagonals bisect each other at 90°.	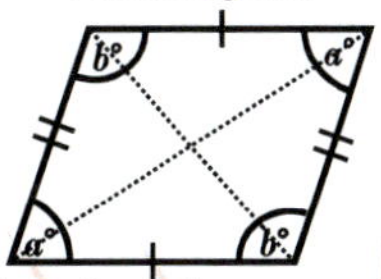 Opposite angles are equal. Opposite sides are parallel and of equal length. The diagonals bisect each other.	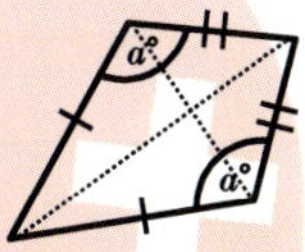 Two of the opposite angles are equal. Two pairs of sides are of equal lengths. The diagonals intersect at 90°.
Regular pentagon	**Regular hexagon**	**Regular heptagon**	**Regular octagon**	**Regular nonagon**
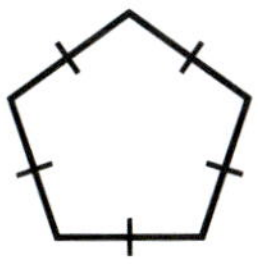 All five angles are equal. All five sides are of equal length. The sum of the interior angles is 540°.	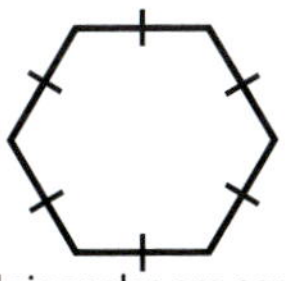 All six angles are equal. All six sides are of equal length. The sum of the interior angles is 720°.	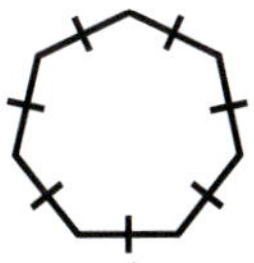 All seven angles are equal. All seven sides are of equal length. The sum of the interior angles is 900°.	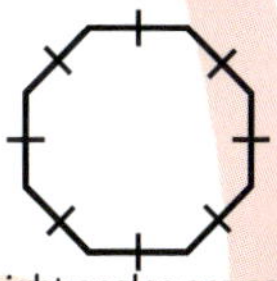 All eight angles are equal. All eight sides are of equal length. The sum of the interior angles is 1,080°.	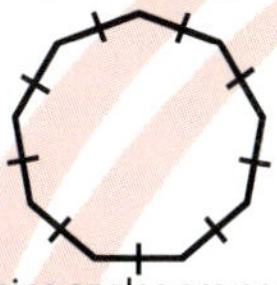 All nine angles are equal. All nine sides are of equal length. The sum of the interior angles is 1,260°.

3D Shapes

Figures with three dimensions: length, width and depth.

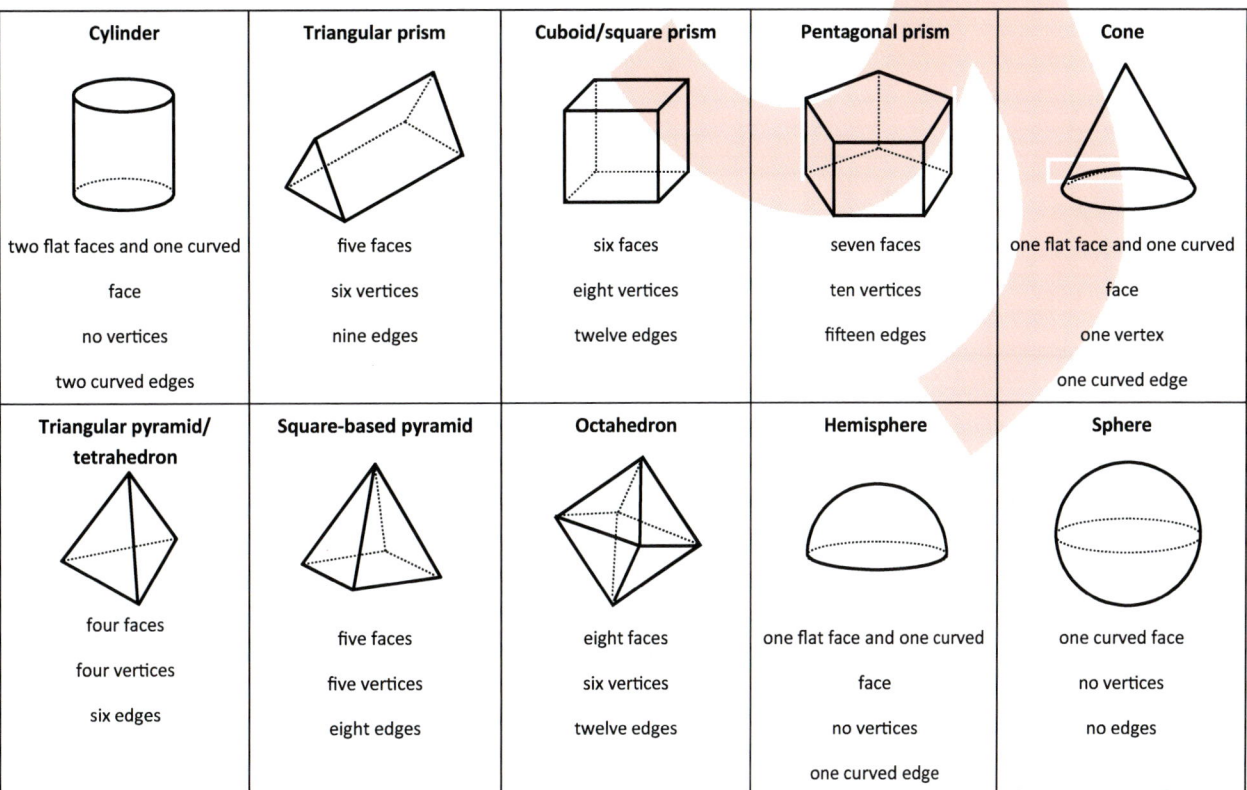

Cylinder	Triangular prism	Cuboid/square prism	Pentagonal prism	Cone
two flat faces and one curved face no vertices two curved edges	five faces six vertices nine edges	six faces eight vertices twelve edges	seven faces ten vertices fifteen edges	one flat face and one curved face one vertex one curved edge
Triangular pyramid/ tetrahedron	**Square-based pyramid**	**Octahedron**	**Hemisphere**	**Sphere**
four faces four vertices six edges	five faces five vertices eight edges	eight faces six vertices twelve edges	one flat face and one curved face no vertices one curved edge	one curved face no vertices no edges

Area Formulae

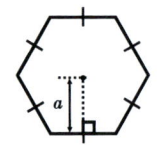

Area of a regular polygon = ¹/₂ × apothem × perimeter
= ¹/₂ × a × p

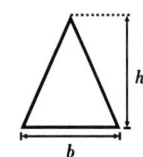

Area of a triangle = ¹/₂ × base × perpendicular height
= ¹/₂ × b × h

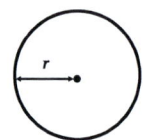

Area of a circle = pi × radius²
= $\pi \times r^2$

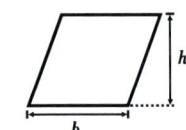

Area of a parallelogram = base × perpendicular height
= $b \times h$

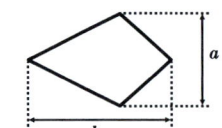

Area of a kite = ¹/₂ × product of the two diagonals
= ¹/₂ × a × b

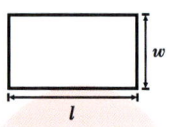

Area of a quadrilateral = length × width
= $l \times w$

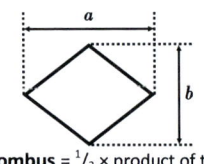

Area of a rhombus = ¹/₂ × product of the two diagonals
= ¹/₂ × a × b

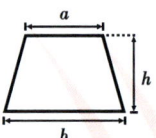

Area of a trapezium = ¹/₂ × sum of the lengths of the parallel sides × perpendicular height
= ¹/₂ × ($a + b$) × h

Volume Formulae

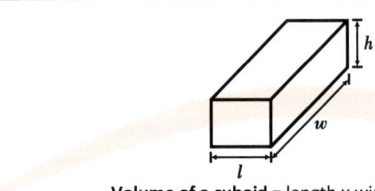

Volume of a cuboid = length × width × height
= $l \times w \times h$

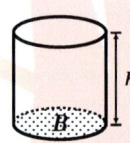

Volume of a prism = area of cross-section × height
= $B \times h$

Other Useful Formulae

Surface area of a 3D shape = sum of the areas of all the faces	Perimeter of a 2D shape = sum of the lengths of all the sides

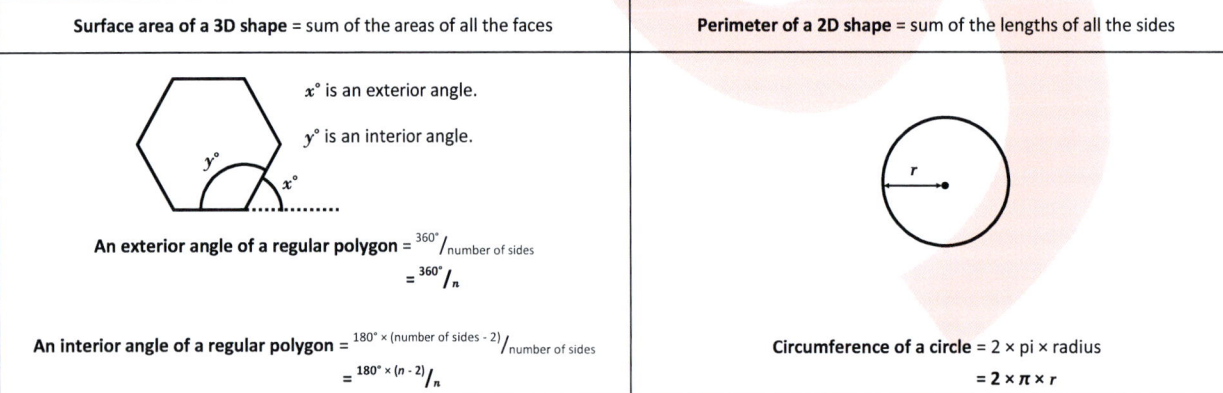

$x°$ is an exterior angle.

$y°$ is an interior angle.

An exterior angle of a regular polygon = ³⁶⁰°/number of sides
= ³⁶⁰°/n

An interior angle of a regular polygon = ¹⁸⁰° × (number of sides - 2)/number of sides
= ¹⁸⁰° × (n - 2)/n

Circumference of a circle = 2 × pi × radius
= $2 \times \pi \times r$

Probability

A measure of how likely it is that a particular event will occur.

The probability of event A happening, P(A), is given by: number of ways in which event A can happen ÷ total number of possible outcomes.

'And' rule	'Or' rule
The 'and' rule is used to find the probability of a combination of events occurring. The probability of events A **and** B happening is: P(A and B) = P(A) × P(B) The word 'and' is replaced by a multiplication sign.	The 'or' rule is used to find the probability of one or other event occurring. The probability of event A **or** B happening is: P(A or B) = P(A) + P(B) The word 'or' is replaced by an addition sign.

Tree diagram

One way of illustrating the probabilities of different events occurring is by using branches on a tree diagram. Each branch represents one possible event and is labelled with its probability.

e.g. a tree diagram illustrating two tosses of an unbiased coin

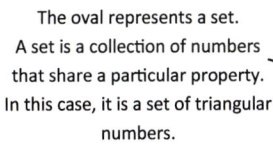

You can use the 'and' rule and the 'or' rule with the tree diagram: multiply probabilities along the branches, and add probabilities down the columns.

Probability scale

A scale that ranges from zero to one and measures the likelihood of an event occurring.

impossible   improbable   equally likely   probable   certain

0   0.25   0.5   0.75   1

Picking out a black marble from a bag which contains only blue marbles

A fair coin landing on heads

Picking out a red marble from a bag which contains only red marbles

Remember that probabilities can be expressed as fractions, decimals or percentages.

Venn Diagrams

A diagram showing all logical relations for a collection of sets using overlapping ovals, non-overlapping ovals and a rectangular boundary.

The oval represents a set. A set is a collection of numbers that share a particular property. In this case, it is a set of triangular numbers.

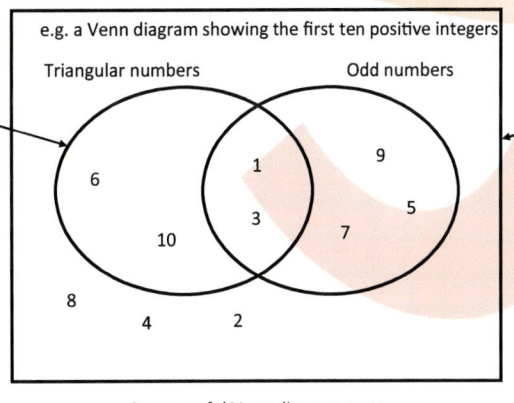

e.g. a Venn diagram showing the first ten positive integers

The rectangle represents the universal set. The universal set contains all the elements in the sets within it. In this case, it is the set of the first ten positive integers.

Some useful Venn diagram patterns:

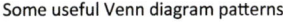

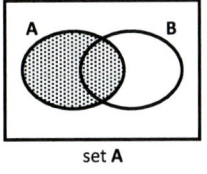

set **A**

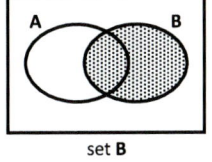

set **B**

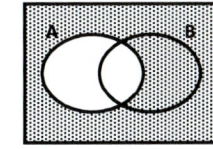

not **A**

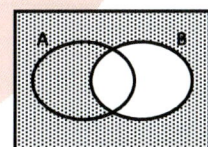

not **B**

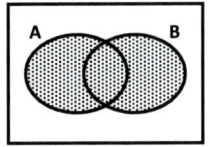

A or **B**

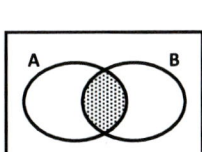

A and **B**

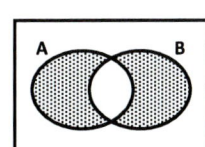

only **A** or only **B**

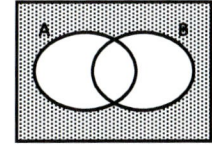

not **A** and not **B**

Instructions

Write your answers on the answer lines provided as shown below:

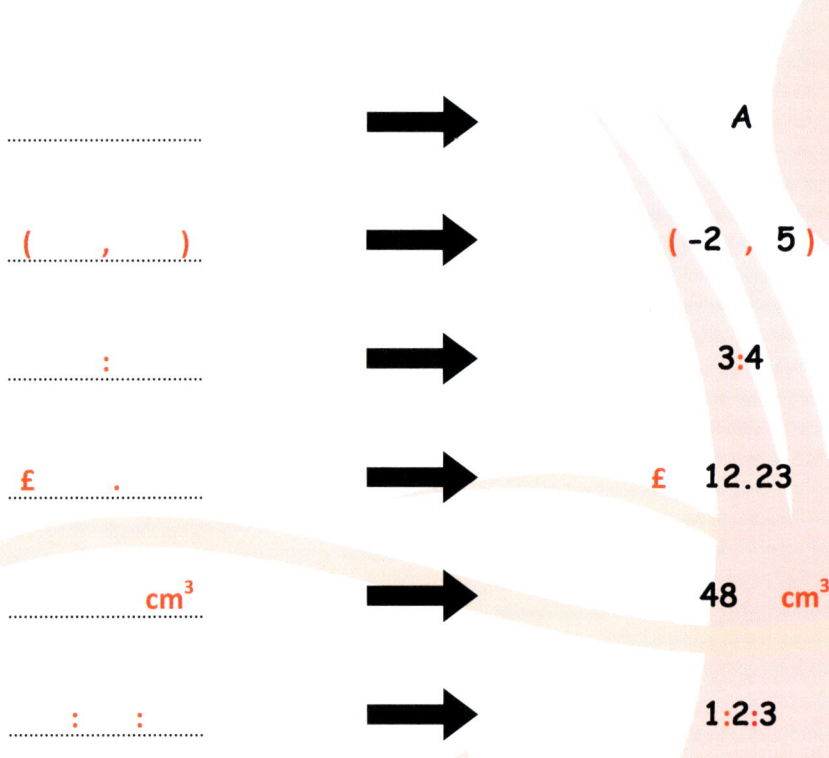

.... ➡ *A*

(...... , ...) ➡ (-2 , 5)

.... : .... ➡ 3 : 4

£ .... ➡ £ 12.23

.... cm³ ➡ 48   cm³

.... : .... : .... ➡ 1:2:3

Chapter 1

Four Operations

Chapter 1: Four Operations - Beginner

1. Prasha bought a pair of shoes for £47 and a coat for £86. How much did she spend altogether?

£ _____ . _____

2. In the number pyramid puzzle below, the number in each box is equal to the sum of the numbers in the two boxes below it. What is the value of the number in the top box?

```
        ?
     [  ][  ]
  [102][  ][58]
[43][  ][  ][27]
```

....

3. A bus with 23 passengers stops at a bus stop. A total of 7 passengers get off the bus and 34 get on. How many passengers are on the bus when it leaves the stop?

....

4. A small theatre has nine rows of seating with eight chairs in each row. If the theatre doubles its seating capacity by building an extension, how many seats will the theatre then have?

....

5. An electronics shop has 10 identical laptop computers on sale at a total cost of £4,386. What is the price of two laptop computers?

£ _____ . _____

6. Guwon writes down a number on a card. He divides the number by 6 and then multiplies the result by 8, giving a final answer of 24. What number did Guwon write on the card?

....

7. A bookcase has eight shelves. Half the shelves have 12 fiction books on each shelf and the remaining shelves have nine non-fiction books on each. How many books are in the bookcase?

....

8. John gives $\frac{1}{3}$ of his 24 marbles to his friend Hal. Hal then buys a bag of 12 marbles to add to his collection. How many marbles has Hal got altogether?

9. When multiplied together, the three numbers in each row equal 60. The three numbers in each column add up to the numbers shown below the grid. What number should replace the question mark?

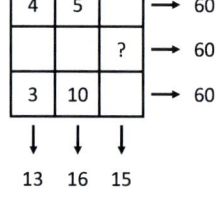

....

10. Farida thinks of a number and divides it by 4. After subtracting 1 from the result, her final answer is 2. What number did Farida originally think of?

....

11. Use the rules of combined operations to work out the result of the following sum:

$$48 - 7 \times 5 + 14$$

....

12. The length of a rectangle is four times its width. If its length is 48cm, what is the distance around the outside of the rectangle?

_____ cm

13. In the equation below, the same single-digit number must be placed in both boxes to balance the equation. What is the missing number?

$$6 \times \boxed{?} + 4 = 9 \times \boxed{?} - 17$$

....

14. Jane sells three-quarters of her 120 cakes at the school fete and half the remaining cakes to her friends. How many cakes are left unsold?

....

15. Use the rules of combined operations to work out the result of the following sum:

$$(84 - 63) \div 7 + 26$$

....

Chapter 1: Four Operations - Intermediate

1. What is the difference between 263 and 642?

   ....

2. Both positive and negative numbers are used in the number grid below. The sum of each row and each column is the same. What number should replace the question mark?

		?
6	2	
1	–4	5

   ....

3. A music shop has 265 CDs for sale. On the first day, 39 CDs are sold. On the following day, 56 new CDs are delivered and also put on sale. How many CDs are on sale after the second day delivery?

   ....

4. What number, when multiplied by 10,000, gives an answer of 400,000?

   ....

5. Niki places blocks across a table top which is 1m 20cm wide. The blocks are placed end-to-end and are each 4cm wide. How many blocks are needed to cover the width of the table top?

   ....

6. Ahmed cubes the number 2 and then multiplies the answer by the square root of 36. Finally, Ahmed divides the result by 4 squared. What is Ahmed's final answer?

   ....

7. Adele purchases seven pens for £1.75 each and five erasers priced at 87p each. How much does Adele pay in total?

   £ ....

8. Use the rules of combined operations to work out the result of:

   $(17 – 9) × 11 + 8000$

   ....

9. Kushal has 228 stickers to put in his empty sticker album. He puts the maximum of 16 stickers on each page until he gets to the last page. How many stickers will Kushal have on the last page?

   ....

10. The cost of six colour ink cartridges is £75.60. Ayesha buys one colour cartridge and pays with a £20 note. How much change does Ayesha get back?

    £ ....

11. A food shop has 11 boxes of Crumbo biscuits and each box holds 12 packets of biscuits. In one week, 42 packets of Crumbo biscuits are sold, and in the second week 52 packets are sold. How many packets are left unsold at the end of the second week?

    ....

12. The unknown number C is common to both of the equations shown below. What is the answer R in equation 2?

Equation 1	6	×	9	–		=	47
					C		
Equation 2	24	÷	8	+		=	R

    ....

13. Use the rules of combined operations to work out the result of:

    $(130 – 39) ÷ (4 + 3)$

    ....

14. A bed can be bought for cash at a cost of £640. Alternatively, the customer can pay an £85 deposit and 24 monthly payments of £27.50. How much does the customer save using the cash payment method?

    £ ....

15. For the equations below, what is the result of Q – P?

    $P = 14 – 5 × 2 + 8$ $Q = –2 + 18 ÷ 6 + 16$

    ....

1. What is the sum of 287,988 and 306,745?

   ....

2. In one year, a supermarket sold 4,837 tins of tomato soup and 2,968 tins of chicken soup. How many more tins of tomato soup were sold compared to tins of chicken soup?

   ....

3. The table below gives the distances between three world cities. What is the difference in distance between travelling from London to New Delhi direct and travelling from London to New Delhi via Cairo?

From	To	Distance (km)
London	Cairo	3,513
Cairo	New Delhi	4,429
London	New Delhi	6,718

   .... km

4. A jar holds 520g of pickles. The jars are packed in boxes of 12 and loaded into crates of 50 boxes. What is the weight of pickles in one full crate, expressed in kilograms?

   .... kg

5. 42 theatre tickets cost £1,029. What does each ticket cost?

   £ ....

6. Tom cuts a 2.16m baton of wood into nine equal length pieces. How long is each piece expressed in centimetres?

   .... cm

7. A dining set consisting of a table and six matching chairs is on sale. The table is priced at £234.99 and each chair is £48.75. What is the total cost of the dining set?

   £ ....

8. A giraffe weighs 1,600kg and an elephant is 140,000 times the weight of a 45g golf ball. What is the combined weight of one giraffe and one elephant, expressed in kilograms?

   .... kg

9. A water tank holds 420,000ml of water when full. If the tank is only $^7/_8$ full, what is the quantity of water in the tank, expressed in litres?

   l

10. Mrs Singh pays £153 for 34 identical toys to sell in her shop. To make a profit, she adds £1.90 to the price she paid for each toy. For how much does Mrs Singh sell each toy?

    £ ....

11. Use the rules of combined operations to work out the result of:

    $$(3 + 9) \times 7 - 18 \div 3$$

    ....

12. A rectangular shaped swimming pool has a length of 12.8m. The distance around all four sides of the pool is 34m. What is the area of the pool?

    .... m²

13. In the equation below, what number must replace the question mark in order to balance the equation?

    $$38 - 3 \times 5 = \boxed{?} \div 4 + 14$$

    ....

14. The number 7 is multiplied by the second cube number and 4 is added to the result. The answer is then divided by the third triangular number. What is the final result?

    ....

15. Nine large cakes are each cut into eighths, ready to be sold for 68p a slice at the school fete. Sales of the cake slices by the end of the fete amounted to £41.48. How many cakes were left unsold, expressed as a decimal number?

    ....

Chapter 2

Number Values and Sequences

1. Write the number *seven thousand, two hundred and ninety-eight* in figures.

2. The length of a room is measured in millimetres for accuracy and found to be 10,003mm. What is the number 10,003 in words?

3. Write the set of numbers below in ascending order.

   55,616   56,516   56,165   55,661   55,605

4. Maathu writes the number *four thousand, two hundred and six* in words correctly on a piece of paper. He then asks his sister, Vinnie, to write the same number in figures underneath it. Unfortunately, Vinnie writes the number incorrectly as 42,006. What should Vinnie have written in figures?

5. Kamal buys a new car for £14,738. In the price, how many pounds is the 4 worth?

   £

6. In the breakdown of the number 27,649 below, what is the value of the missing number?

   $27649 = \boxed{?} + 7000 + 600 + 40 + 9$

7. Jacob weighs 68.72kg. Round Jacob's weight to the nearest kilogram.

   kg

8. What is the number 94.63 to the nearest tenth?

9. The rule for finding the nth pattern in a sequence is $9n$. What is the value of the 8th pattern?

10. How many smiley faces are needed to create pattern 5 in the sequence below?

    Pattern 1   Pattern 2   Pattern 3

11. What is the rule for finding the nth pattern of circles in the sequence below?

    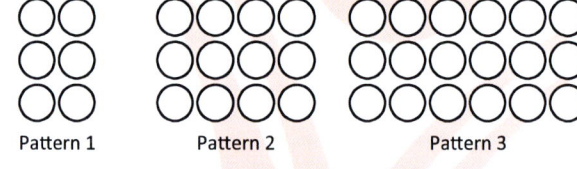

    Pattern 1   Pattern 2   Pattern 3

12. What is the missing number in the sequence below?

    −14   ?   0   7   14   21   28

13. The rule for finding the nth term in the sequence below is in the form of: $\boxed{?} - \boxed{?}\, n$. Write down the full rule for the nth term.

    5   0   −5   −10   −15

14. How many squares in total are needed to create patterns 5 and 6 in the sequence?

    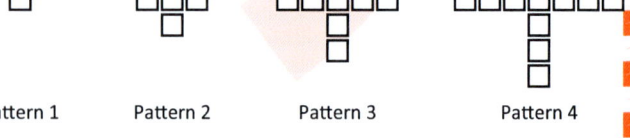

    Pattern 1   Pattern 2   Pattern 3   Pattern 4

15. What is the value of the next term in the sequence below?

    1.01   1.03   1.05   1.07   1.09   ?

1. What is the number *four hundred and twenty-six thousand, nine hundred and thirty-eight* expressed in figures?

....

2. A newly built office block has 730,805 square metres of floor space to rent. Write the number 730,805 in words.

....

3. What is the third largest in the set of numbers below?

338,308   330,893   338,039   309,839   338,903

....

4. Add 400,000 to the number 28,012.

....

5. A house is advertised for sale at a price of £585,495. What is the value of the digit 8 in the number 585,495?

....

6. Write the number 321.416 correct to two decimal places.

....

7. The price of an expensive television is 100 times that of a £29.45 camera. What is the price of the television rounded to the nearest £1,000?

£ ....

8. How many squares in total are required to create patterns 5 and 7 in the sequence below?

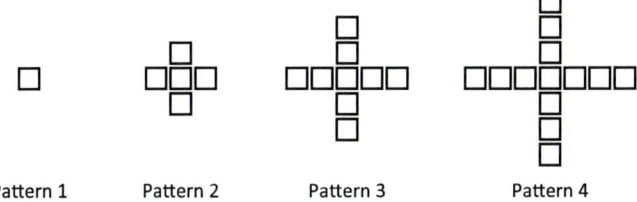

Pattern 1   Pattern 2   Pattern 3   Pattern 4

9. Adele divided 7,007 by a number N and obtained an answer of 700,700. What was the divisor number N?

....

10. What is the rule for finding the nth term in the sequence of numbers below?

3   5   7   9   11

11. The nth term rule for a sequence of numbers is $5n - 4$. What is the result of subtracting the 5th term value from the 6th term value?

....

12. What is the value of the missing term in the sequence below?

$\frac{3}{8}$ $\frac{7}{8}$ $1\frac{3}{8}$? $2\frac{3}{8}$

....

13. The diagram below shows a pattern of shaded and unshaded circles. If the pattern was repeated, would the 29th circle be shaded or unshaded?

● ● ○ ○ ○ ○ ○

....

14. In a descending number sequence, subtracting 4 from a term gives the value of the next term. If the 5th term is −3, what is the value of the 1st term?

....

15. What is the next term in the sequence below?

1   2   4   3   9   5   16   7   ?

....

1. The distance from the Earth to the Sun is around 92,955,807 miles. Write this number of miles in words.

....

2. What is the sum of the second and third largest numbers in the set below?

3313031 3331131 3313113 3113113 3313133

....

3. One particularly large modern oil tanker carries *eighty-three million, seven hundred and four thousand, six hundred and three* gallons of oil. Write this number in figures.

....

4. What is the value of the underlined digit in the number below?

6<u>4</u>5,037,189

....

5. Farida subtracts 518,238,650 from 718,238,650 and then subtracts 1,000,000 from 1,950,000. What is the sum of the two answers from Farida's calculations?

....

6. Sam's milkman delivers 126,878 bottles of milk in a year. Sam rounds the number of bottles to the nearest 100 and then finds the difference between the rounded and actual number delivered in one year. What should Sam's final answer be?

....

7. Jane writes the number 3.14159 to three decimal places of accuracy. What should Jane's answer be?

....

8. Sanjay rounds both the diameter of the Sun (864,938 miles) and the diameter of the Earth (7,926 miles) to the nearest 100. He then divides his rounded answers to discover how many whole planet Earths can be fitted along the diameter of the Sun. What should Sanjay's final answer be?

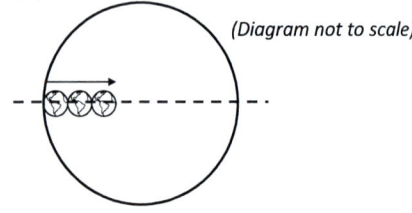

(Diagram not to scale)

9. Look at the sequence of circle patterns below. How many circles are needed to create the 27th pattern?

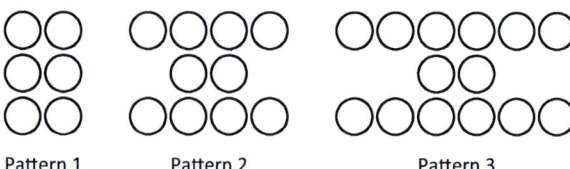

Pattern 1   Pattern 2   Pattern 3

....

10. For the pattern sequence in Q9 above, which pattern number has 142 circles?

....

11. What is the missing first term in the number sequence below?

?   −18   −11   −4   3

....

12. The nth rule applying to a sequence is $\frac{3n}{5}$. What is the value of the 6th term expressed in mixed number format?

....

13. Write down the rule for the number of sticks in the pattern sequence below. Express your answer in terms of pattern number, n.

Pattern 1   Pattern 2   Pattern 3

....

14. The triangles below are part of a repeating pattern. What capital letter will be on the 86th triangle?

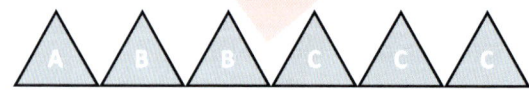

....

15. What is the next term in the sequence below?

1   1   3   2   6   4   10   8   15   16   ?

....

FIRST PAST THE POST

Chapter 3

Factors and Multiples

1. Write down a number between 21 and 29 that divides exactly into 300.

    ....

2. Write down all the factors of 6.

    ....

3. How many of the numbers in the grid below are factors of 24?

8	36	48
9	24	1
15	3	10

    ....

4. For the numbers 10 and 15, what are the common factors?

    ....

5. Three of the six factors of 12 are shown in the pyramid of squares below. What is the sum of the remaining three factors missing from the bottom row?

    ```
          6
       1     4
     ?    ?    ?
    ```

    ....

6. What is the highest common factor (HCF) of 6 and 9?

    ....

7. Which multiple of 9 is between 47 and 61?

    ....

8. The 29 houses down one side of Wood Street are evenly numbered as shown below. What is the number of the last house on the same side of the street?

    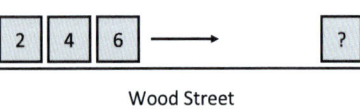

    Wood Street

    ....

9. What is the sum of the first three multiples of 7?

    ....

10. Eight of the first nine multiples of a number are shown in the grid squares below. What is the missing multiple in the centre square?

72	16	48
32	?	56
40	24	64

    ....

11. Bottles of still water are sealed into plastic packs of 6 and then loaded into boxes, each containing 10 packs. How many bottles are there in four boxes?

    ....

12. What is the lowest common multiple (LCM) of 3 and 5?

    ....

13. Which one of the following numbers is a factor of 16 and a multiple of 4?

    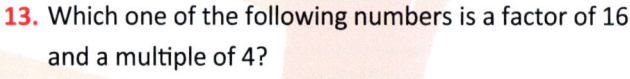

    2   6   12   8   20

    ....

14. Two factors of 18 and two multiples of 3 are shown in the incomplete table below. What are the four numbers missing from the shaded cell?

Factors of 18	1, 2
Multiples of 3	12, 15
Numbers that are both factors of 18 and multiples of 3	?

    ....

15. Number N is between 8 and 40. N is a factor of 45 and a multiple of 5. What is number N?

    ....

1. Write down all the factors of 54.

   ....

2. Which of the numbers below are composite numbers? Circle your answer(s).

   432   127   980   289   479   1885   263

3. The common factors for the numbers 36 and 48 are positioned in the grid below to form the shape of a capital letter. Which capital letter is it?

4	12	3
16	2	8
36	6	24
9	1	18

   ....

4. Tina writes down the factors of 34 that are prime and adds them together. What answer should Tina obtain?

   ....

5. What is the highest common factor (HCF) of 42 and 56?

   ....

6. Five of the eight factors of 70 are shown in the shape F below. What are the three missing prime factors?

10	?	?
14		
70	?	
1		
35		

   ....

7. Which multiple of 34 is between 138 and 200?

   ....

8. A furniture shop sells chairs in sets of six. Which of the following numbers of chairs make complete sets? Circle your answer(s).

   76   90   124   138   168   184

9. Apples are packed into bags of 12 and placed in boxes each containing 20 bags ready for delivery to the supermarket. If each bag contained only four apples, how many bags would fit in the same size box?

   ....

10. What number is missing from the grid below?

17	34	51
34	51	68
51	68	?

    ....

11. A large restaurant has 40 dining tables. Three-quarters of the tables seat up to four diners and the remaining tables seat up to six. How many diners can be catered for when the restaurant is full?

    ....

12. What is the lowest common multiple (LCM) of 12 and 15?

    ....

13. Which of the following numbers is a factor of 81 and a multiple of 9?

    18   36   28   45   27   54

    ....

14. Look at the incomplete Venn diagram below. What is the 100th multiple of each of the two missing numbers in the centre shaded area?

    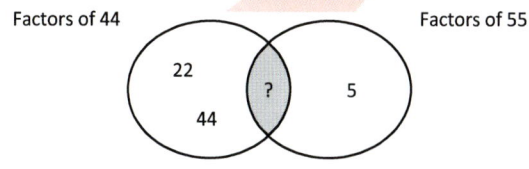

    Factors of 44   Factors of 55

    22
        ?   5
    44

    ....

15. I am a three-digit number less than 130. I am a multiple of both 7 and 9. How many factors do I have?

    ....

1. What are the common factors of 36, 54 and 96?

   ....

2. What are the prime factors of 238?

   ....

3. What are the four numbers missing from the shaded central area of the Venn diagram below?

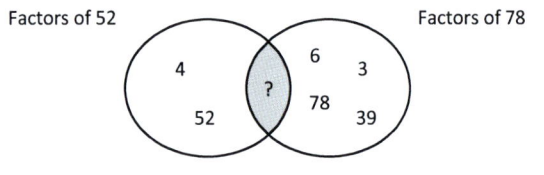

   Factors of 52   Factors of 78

   ....

4. I am a composite number with three different factors that sum to 13. My factors also form a trebling sequence. What number am I?

   ....

5. What is the sum of the two highest common factors (HCFs) missing from the table below?

Number Pairs	HCF
40 and 100	
57 and 76	
SUM	?

   ....

6. Number N has six factors. Four of the factors are 11, 2, 22, and 4. What is the number N?

   ....

7. Which multiple of 83 is between 590 and 730?

   ....

8. A large wedding reception has 12 guests seated at the head table. Other guests fill up the places at 50 other tables. $^4/_5$ of these tables each seat four and the remaining tables each seat six. How many guests are at the reception in total?

   ....

9. What is the lowest common multiple (LCM) of 4, 5 and 8?

   ....

10. The 8th multiple of 84 is the 7th multiple of which number?

    ....

11. Work out the number in the shaded square below.

76	152	228	304
152	228	304	
228	304		
304			?

    ....

12. Work out the lowest common multiple (LCM) of 30 and 42.

    ....

13. I am a number with three digits that add up to 14. I am also the 7th multiple of a number that has eight factors, six of which are 2, 4, 7, 8, 14 and 28. What number am I?

    ....

14. Look at the incomplete Venn diagram below. What is the highest common factor (HCF) of the three numbers missing from the shaded central area?

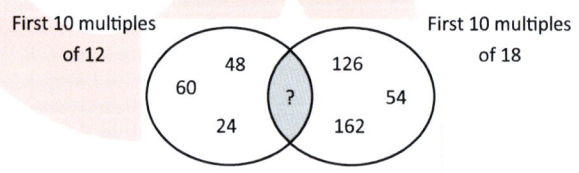

    First 10 multiples of 12   First 10 multiples of 18

    ....

15. Work your way down the table below to find answers (a) to (d).

(a) The highest common factor of 28, 52 and 68	?
(b) The 15th multiple of answer (a)	?
(c) The 3 different prime factors of answer (b)	?
(d) The lowest common multiple of answer (c)	?

    (a) ....   (b) ....

    (c) ....   (d) ....

FIRST PAST THE POST®

Chapter 4

Fractions and Decimals

1. Circle the two equivalent fractions.

   $^1/_2$ $^1/_3$ $^3/_4$ $^3/_5$ $^2/_6$

2. Write down the shaded area of the circle below as a fraction in its lowest terms.

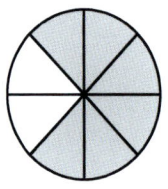

   ....

3. What number should replace the question mark to complete the equivalent pair of fractions shown below?

   $^8/_{12} = {}^2/_?$

   ....

4. Write down both the equivalent fractions shown by the shaded areas below.

 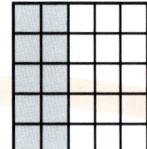

   ....

5. Work out $^1/_2 + {}^1/_3$.

   ....

6. Express the result of the multiplication below as a fraction in its lowest terms.

   $^3/_5 \times {}^2/_3$

   ....

7. Kim bought a camera for £32.76. Express the price Kim paid to the nearest pound.

   £ ....

8. What number should replace the question mark in the multiplication below?

   $\boxed{?} \times 10 = 63.9$

   ....

9. Pierre's bottle of water holds 0.244 litres when full. What is this value to two decimal places of accuracy?

   l

10. What number should replace the question mark in the division below?

    $\boxed{?} \div 100 = 2.58$

    ....

11. A can of tomato soup weighs 0.54 kg. What is the weight of nine cans?

    .... kg

12. Eight tins of paint hold 36.56 litres. What is the capacity of one tin?

    l

13. Express the largest fraction below as a decimal number.

    $^3/_5$ $^1/_2$ $^5/_8$ $^3/_4$ $^2/_3$

    ....

14. What is the sum of the fractions represented by the shaded areas of the diagrams below? Express your final answer in decimal number format.

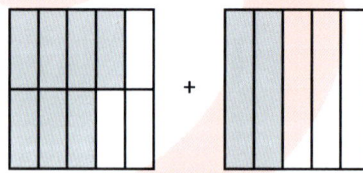

    ....

15. Work out the subtraction below, expressing your final answer as a decimal number.

    $2 \, ^1/_2 - {}^1/_8$

    ....

Chapter 4: Fractions and Decimals - Intermediate

1. Circle the three equivalent fractions.

$^{18}/_{30}$ $^{16}/_{20}$ $^{25}/_{35}$ $^{24}/_{28}$ $^{6}/_{10}$ $^{12}/_{15}$ $^{64}/_{80}$

2. List the 5 shaded areas below as fractions in ascending order of size. Reduce fractions to their lowest terms where necessary.

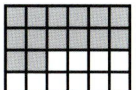 

3. Find the fraction which lies halfway between $^{3}/_{8}$ and $^{1}/_{4}$.

4. Write down both the equivalent fractions shown by the shaded areas below.

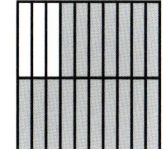 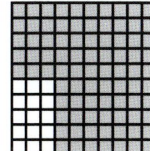

5. Work out the subtraction below, expressing your answer in mixed number format.

$$8 \, ^{3}/_{8} - 5 \, ^{5}/_{8}$$

6. Work out the division below, expressing your answer in its lowest terms.

$$^{6}/_{7} \div 10$$

7. Round 37.096kg to the nearest 100g.

8. Prasha bought a guitar for £73.92 and paid with four £20 notes. How much change did Prasha receive back, to the nearest 10p?

£ ....

9. Work out the following problem:

$$\frac{9.072 \times 10 \times 100 \times 1000}{100 \times 100}$$

10. Lakgana's wardrobe is 2,096mm high. Express this measurement in centimetres (cm), to the nearest cm.

.... cm

11. Given that 1 ft = 0.3048m, what is 5 feet expressed in centimetres?

.... cm

12. Jane has an A4 sheet of paper measuring 21cm by 29.7cm. She cuts the sheet into four equal size pieces as shown below. What is the perimeter of the shaded piece?

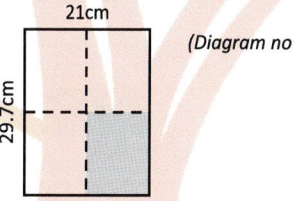

(Diagram not to scale)

.... cm

13. Write the mixed number below as a decimal number.

$$8 \, ^{685}/_{1000}$$

14. $^{3}/_{8}$ of the pages in a book have a picture on them whilst $^{5}/_{16}$ of the pages have two pictures. There are no more than two pictures on a single page.

(a) Express as a decimal the number of pages that have no picture.

(b) If the number of pages in the book is 64, how many pages have no picture?

15. Express 6.42 as an improper fraction in its lowest terms.

Chapter 4: Fractions and Decimals - Advanced

1. Fill in the box below using one of these signs: >, < or = .

$$\frac{5}{9} + \frac{2}{3} \quad \boxed{} \quad \frac{4}{5} + \frac{7}{10}$$

2. Beth cuts 180mm off the end of a strip of wood that is 1.5m in length. Express the amount of wood left on the strip as a fraction of the original total length in its lowest terms.

   ....

3. Work out the subtraction below, expressing your answer as a mixed number in its lowest terms.

$$8 \, ^{225}/_{1000} - 3 \, ^{4}/_{5}$$

   ....

4. Sanjay, Mel and Alex are playing a card game. The incomplete table shows the number of cards held by each player at a particular point in the game. What is the total number of cards held by all three players?

Name	Number of cards held
Sanjay	12
Mel	$^{2}/_{3} \times 12 = ?$
Alex	$1 \, ^{1}/_{6} \times 12 = ?$
	Total = ?

5. What number should replace the question mark below?

$$^{3}/_{5} \text{ of } \boxed{?} = £660$$

   £ ....

6. Work out the problem below, giving your answer in mixed number format.

$$(2 \, ^{2}/_{9} \times 6) \div 4$$

   ....

7. What number should replace the question mark in the number statement below?

$$7.184 - \boxed{?} = 6.784$$

   ....

8. What is the number 84.726439 correct to three decimal places of accuracy?

   ....

9. Farida's living room rug is 2.18m long and 1.1m wide. What is the area of the rug in (a) m^2 and (b) cm^2?

   (a) .... m^2

   (b) .... cm^2

10. A car travels 54 miles in 1 hour at a constant speed. Express the number of miles the car travels in 10 seconds as a decimal.

   .... miles

11. Express the shaded area on the diagram as:

   (a) a mixed number in its simplest form,

   ....

   (b) an improper fraction in its simplest form,

   ....

   (c) a decimal number rounded to 2 decimal places.

   ....

12. What is one fifth of the value, three and a tenth, expressed as a decimal?

   ....

13. Express the number 14.7125 as a mixed number in its lowest terms.

   ....

14. What is the sum of the fractions represented by the shaded areas of the diagrams below? Express your answer in decimal number format to the nearest tenth.

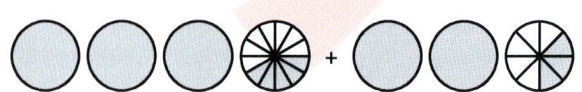

15. Sam bought an ink cartridge for £12.50 and paid with a £20 note. How much change did Sam receive, expressed as a percentage of the £20?

   .... %

Chapter 5

Percentages, Ratios and Proportions

1. Find 10% of 70.

....

2. There are 100 children in a school. 80% are boys. How many are girls?

....

3. A television costs £400. The price is reduced by 5%. What is the reduced price?

£ ....

4. What is 20% of 5kg?

kg ....

5. What percentage of the tiles shown below are shaded?

% ....

6. What is the ratio 6:8 expressed in its lowest terms?

: ....

7. Maya has 21 red beads and 15 blue beads. What is the ratio of red beads to blue beads in its lowest terms?

: ....

8. What is the ratio of shaded to unshaded slices of the pizza in its lowest terms?

: ....

9. The ratio of yellow to green counters in a bag is 4:3. If there are 12 yellow counters, how many green counters are in the bag?

....

10. The following pattern of square cards is repeated along the row until the total number of cards with a cross is 18. How many cards have a dot?

....

11. There are 80 diners in a restaurant. 60 are adults and 20 are children. As a percentage, what proportion of all diners are children?

% ....

12. A cake recipe for 10 people requires 500g of butter. How much butter is needed to create a cake for seven people?

g ....

13. Four in every five people living on a particular street have a mobile phone. There are 100 people living on the street. How many people have a mobile phone?

....

14. A map has a scale of 1cm to 4km. Two cities are 7cm apart on the map. What is the real distance between the cities?

km ....

15. A room plan is drawn to a scale of 1:200. The room is 4cm long in the drawing. What is the real length of the room?

m ....

Chapter 5: Percentages, Ratios and Proportions - Intermediate

1. Find 70% of 600g.

.... g

2. The price of a £15 shirt is increased by 10%. What is the new price?

£ ....

3. Express the fraction $^3/_5$ as a percentage.

.... %

4. A brick wall is shown below. What percentage of bricks are shaded?

.... %

5. 150 tickets are sold for a school play. 50% are sold to adult men, 30% to adult women and the remainder to children. How many tickets are sold to children?

....

6. Sevan purchased 30 postcards. He sent 90% to his friends. How many postcards did he send?

....

7. 12 people in a cafe are drinking tea and 10 people are drinking coffee. What is the ratio of tea to coffee drinkers in its lowest terms?

.... :

8. What is the ratio 42:72 expressed in its lowest terms?

.... :

9. 28 grapes were shared between Farida and John in the ratio of 4:3. How many grapes did John get?

....

10. What is the ratio of shaded to unshaded circles in its lowest terms?

.... :

11. What is the proportion of shaded squares in the pattern below? Express your answer as a fraction in its simplest form.

....

12. A garage sells nine silver cars for every five blue cars. How many blue cars does it sell if it sells 63 silver cars?

....

13. A train travels 8 miles in 16 minutes. How far does it travel in 7 minutes?

.... miles

14. Six packets of biscuits cost £7.50. Packets of these biscuits are also sold by the box for £45. How many packets are in a full box?

....

15. A map is drawn to a scale of 1:2000. How many centimetres would a line representing a distance of 140m be on the map?

.... cm

Chapter 5: Percentages, Ratios and Proportions - Advanced

1. Express the fraction $^{201}/_{300}$ as a percentage.

   .... %

2. Carla spends 72% of her £15 savings on a computer game. How much does Carla spend on the game?

   £ ....

3. 3% of a number N gives a result of 0.27. What is the number N?

   ....

4. Sai cuts her birthday cake into equal pieces as shown below. Sai and her friend Krupa each eat $^1/_8$ of the cake and Sai's other guests at the party eat a further $^7/_{16}$. What percentage of the cake is left uneaten?

   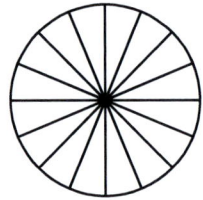

   .... %

5. Esme has £720 in a bank account that pays 2.6% interest. After the interest is paid in, how much money will Esme still need to afford a holiday costing £750?

   £ ....

6. Write the ratio 2:6:14 in its lowest terms.

   .... : ....

7. A 1.5m plank of wood is cut into three lengths L1, L2 and L3. L1 = 65cm and L2 = 45cm. What is the ratio L1 to L2 to L3 expressed in its lowest terms?

   .... : ....

8. What is the ratio of the weights of parcels P1 to P2 expressed in its lowest terms?

   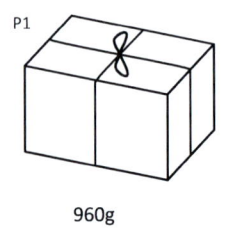
   960g

   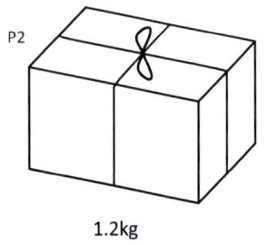
   1.2kg

   .... : ....

9. John is 15 years old, Mario is $^3/_5$ of John's age, and Asha is 80% of John's age. Write down the ratio of John's age to Mario's age to Asha's age in its lowest terms.

   .... : .... : ....

10. Songyo watched television for 1 hour. During the hour, 48 minutes of sport was shown and the remaining time was devoted to adverts. Write down, as a percentage, the proportion of time Songyo was watching adverts.

    .... %

11. 28 litres of water is escaping from a burst pipe every 20 seconds. How much water will escape from the pipe in 1 minute 10 seconds?

    l

12. The row of shapes below is used to create a repeating pattern. How many triangles must be included to create a row of 144 shapes?

    ....

13. The ratio of staff to customers in a department store is 3:14. If there are 42 members of staff, how many people are in the store altogether?

    ....

14. The distance between the towns of Marford and Densley on the map below is 8.5cm. What is the real distance between the towns?

    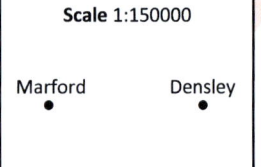

    Scale 1:150000   *(Diagram not to scale)*

    Marford   Densley

    .... km

15. The real distance between two cities is 31.25km. On a scaled map the same cities are shown 12.5cm apart. What is the map scale?

    .... : ....

Chapter 6

Algebra and Number Machines

Chapter 6: Algebra and Number Machines - Beginner

1. If $x + 5 = 6$, what is the value of x?

....

2. If $3a = 18$, what is the value of a?

....

3. A number is cubed, giving a result of 8. What is the original number?

....

4. If $y = 2$ and $z = 5$, solve $2(z - y)$.

....

5. A square is shown below. What is the expression for the area of the square?

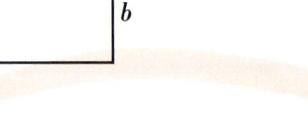

....

6. What number when divided by 4 gives an answer of 5?

....

7. Chris divides a certain amount of money equally between three people. Each person receives £10.50. How much money did Chris originally have?

£ ....

8. What is the value of $1234x$ when $x = 0.1$?

....

9. $4c - 14 = -3c$. What is the value of c?

....

10. Using the equation $y = 12 - 3x$, what is the value of A in the table?

x	3	4	15
y	3	A	−33

....

11. What is the output of the number machine below?

....

12. What is the output of the number machine below?

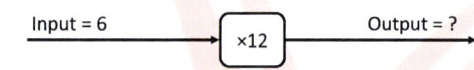

....

13. What is the input to the number machine below?

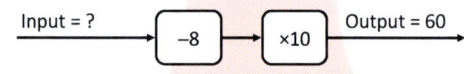

....

14. What is the output of the number machine below?

....

15. What is the output of the number machine below?

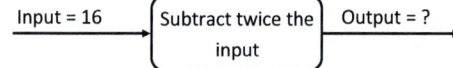

....

1. Solve the equation $x \div 3 - 9 = 12$.

....

2. Emma is 2 years younger than Lin, but 5 years older than Hiten. If Lin is 21 years old, how old is Hiten?

....

3. Three times y, plus eighteen equals fifty-four. What is the value of y?

....

4. If $p = 0.5$ and $q = 1.5$, solve $p(3q - 4p)$.

....

5. What is the simplified expression for the perimeter of the rectangle below?

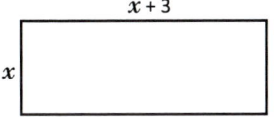

....

6. $14b + 23 = 8b - 13$. What is the value of b?

....

7. £14.80 is to be split between three people. Claire will receive £3.40, Joel will receive £4.85 and Ann will receive the rest. How much will Ann receive?

£ ....

8. The wooden shelves below are 100cm in height. The spacing between all shelves is equal at 20cm. All the shelves themselves are also equal in height. What is the height of one wooden shelf?

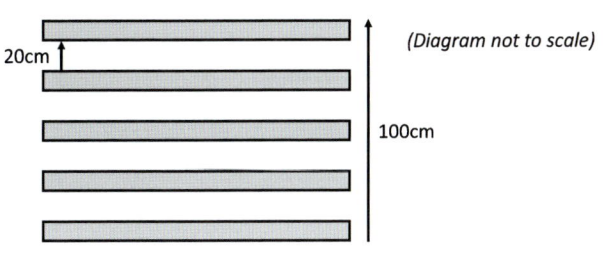

(Diagram not to scale)

20cm

100cm

.... cm

9. On the card below $t = 7$ and the value of s is unknown. The total values of all five letters is given at the bottom of the card. What is the value of s?

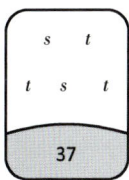

....

10. If $3w - w = 4(2 - x)$, what is the value of w when $x = -1$?

....

11. A function machine adds 9 to the input number and multiplies the result by 11 to get the output. The input is 4. What is the output number?

....

12. What is the output of the number machine below?

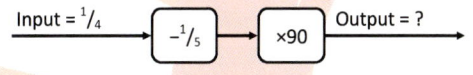

Input = $\frac{1}{4}$ $-\frac{1}{5}$ $\times 90$ Output = ?

....

13. What is the input to the number machine below?

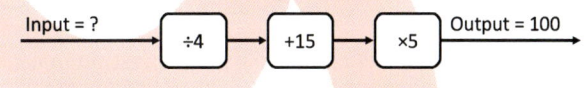

Input = ? $\div 4$ $+15$ $\times 5$ Output = 100

....

14. What is the output of the number machine below?

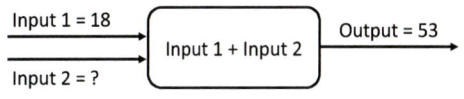

Input = 35 -3^3 $+\sqrt{121}$ Output = ?

....

15. What is the value of input 2 to the number machine below?

Input 1 = 18
Input 2 = ?   Input 1 + Input 2   Output = 53

....

Chapter 6: Algebra and Number Machines - Advanced

1. Give an expression for the perimeter of the shape below.

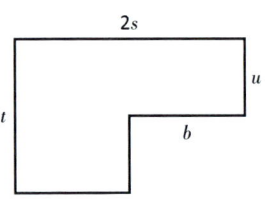

2. $z = (2a - b)(b + 3c)$. What is the value of z if $a = 0.75$, $b = 0.65$ and $c = 0.25$?

3. What is the expression for the output of the number machine below?

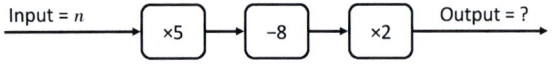

4. What is the value of x in the following equation?

$$41x - 197 = 34 - 113x$$

5. Andreas had x pounds. He gave one fifth of this to his niece and two thirds of this to his daughter. His daughter received £70.50. How much less money did his niece receive compared to his daughter?

£ ....

6. What number is represented by the question mark in the number machine below?

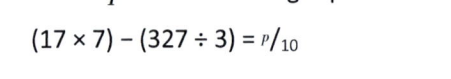

7. What is the value of p in the following expression?

$$(17 \times 7) - (327 \div 3) = {}^p/_{10}$$

8. What is the value of y in the equation, ${}^7/_8 y - 1\,{}^5/_8 = {}^3/_4$? Express your answer as an improper fraction.

9. What number should replace the question mark in the expression below?

$$1340 + 1340 + 1340 + 1340 = ? \times 100$$

10. What is the input to the number machine below?

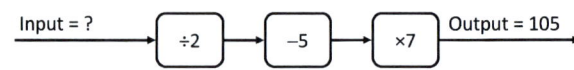

11. Give an expression for the area of the shape below, using only the terms c and b.

12. A negative number when doubled and then squared is 144. What is the number?

13. What is the output of the number machine below?

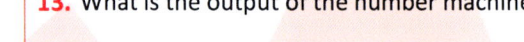

14. What is the simplified expression for the perimeter of the shape below?

15. What is the output of the number machine below?

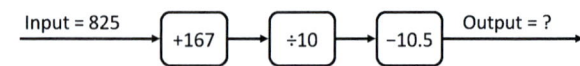

FIRST PAST THE POST®

Chapter 7

Averages and Representing Data

Chapter 7: Averages and Representing Data - Beginner

1. The sum of four numbers is 8. What is the average?

....

2. The following scores were achieved in a Maths test. What was the mode score?

20%   18%   70%   20%   45%   58%   45%   20%

.... %

Ali has the following counters on his table. Using this information, answer questions 3 to 6 .

3. What is the mean?

....

4. What is the median?

....

5. What is the mode?

....

6. What is the range?

....

7. In the table below, five people were asked how many CDs they owned. What was the median number of CDs?

Name	Sapna	Jason	Saud	Anne	Peter
Number of CDs	9	19	12	14	11

....

8. Over five consecutive days, a car travelled the following distances. What was the mean distance covered per day?

Day	Distance (km)
Monday	11
Tuesday	2
Wednesday	14
Thursday	8
Friday	5

.... km

9. 24 people were asked how many pets they have. The results are summarised in the pie chart below. How many people have no pets?

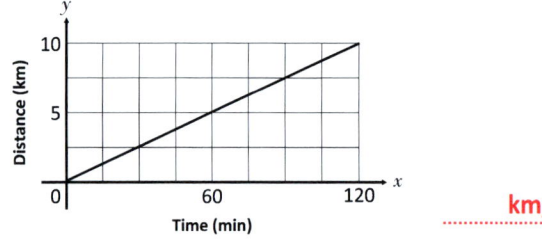

Key:
■ No pets
□ One pet
▨ More than one pet

....

10. What is the average speed in kilometres per hour?

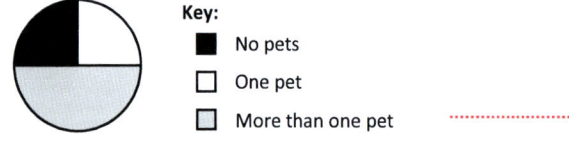

.... km/h

11. The test scores for five people are shown in the chart below. How many people scored more than 10?

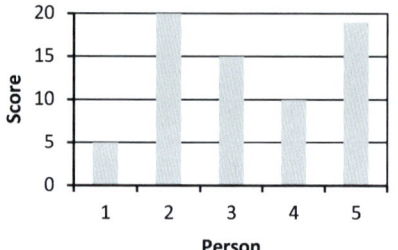

....

12. The tally table below shows the results of a survey which asked people what their favourite colour was. How many people selected blue as their favourite colour? Complete the table.

Colour	Tally	Frequency
Green	~~IIII~~ ~~IIII~~ II	12
Red	~~IIII~~ I	6
Blue	~~IIII~~ ~~IIII~~ ~~IIII~~ I	
Yellow	~~IIII~~ ~~IIII~~	10

13. A school class were asked if they liked Rounders (R) and Volleyball (V). The results are shown in the Venn Diagram. How many pupils were in the class?

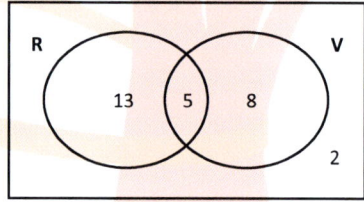

....

14. The highest temperatures were recorded on six days and are shown on the chart. On what percentage of days did the temperature stay under 15°C?

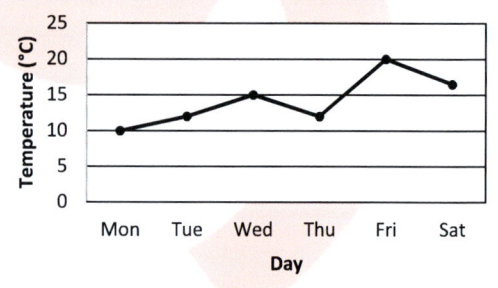

.... %

15. The chart below shows the number of properties sold per type over a two month period. What was the combined number of detached houses and flats sold?

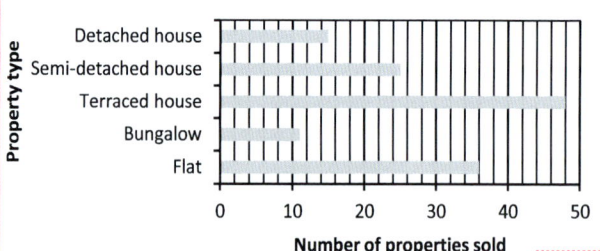

....

1. Eight people scored the following on a science test. A ninth person scored X marks. The mean score was 12. What score did the ninth person receive?

    13   8   1   20   15   16   10   17

    ....

2. These are the lengths of five screws. What is the range?

    3.2cm   2.9cm   3.4cm   4.2cm   3.9cm

    .... cm

The following temperatures were recorded in the last week of January. Using this information, answer questions 3 to 6.

Day	Mon	Tue	Wed	Thu	Fri	Sat	Sun
°C	2	−1	−1	2	3	−1	3

3. What is the mean?   .... °C

4. What is the median?   .... °C

5. What is the mode?   .... °C

6. What is the range?   .... °C

7. Abi buys the items in the table. What was the price of one toothbrush?

Bathroom item	Price per item	Number required	Total price
Soap	£0.40	5	£2.00
Towel	£4.20	4	£16.80
Toothbrush	?	3	?
		Total	£21.50

£ ....

8. A group of people in Spain were asked if they had visited the three countries on the Venn diagram. How many people had been to at least one of Poland or Mexico?

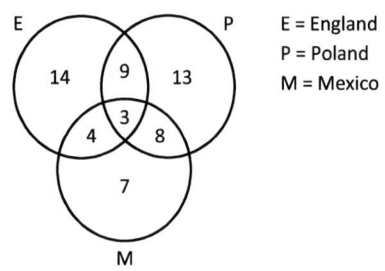

E = England
P = Poland
M = Mexico

....

9. The tally table shows the number of cars owned per person for a set of people. What fraction of people owned more than one car?

Number of cars	Tally	Frequency
0	ЖЖ IIII	14
1	ЖЖ II	12
2	Ж	5
3	III	?

10. The pictogram shows the number of visitors to a museum. How many more people visited on the weekend than on Friday?

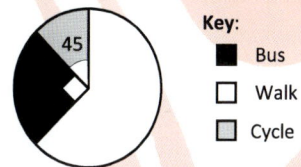

Museum Visitors	
Wed	☺ ☺ ◖
Thu	☺ ☺ ☺ ◖
Fri	☺ ◖ ◖
Sat	☺ ☺ ☺ ◖
Sun	☺ ☺ ☺ ☺

Key:
☺ equals 200 visitors

....

11. 96 children were asked how they travelled to school that morning. The results are shown in the pie chart. How many children walked to school?

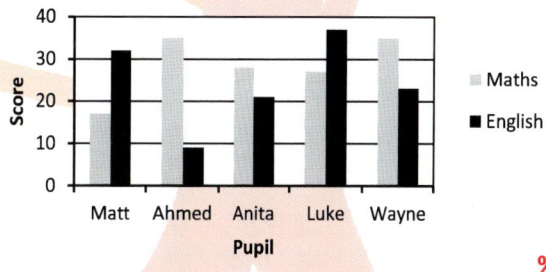

Key:
■ Bus
☐ Walk
▨ Cycle

....

12. The chart shows English and Maths test results for five pupils. What percentage of pupils scored a higher result in English than in Maths?

Score / Pupil: Matt, Ahmed, Anita, Luke, Wayne

☐ Maths
■ English

.... %

13. Find the mode of the following values.

    25g   0.25kg   25,000mg   250g   0.025kg

    .... g

14. Train A travels at a speed of 50km/h for 3 hours whilst train B travels at a speed of 65km/h for the same amount of time. What is the average speed of the two trains?

    .... km/h

15. The chart shows temperatures over six days. How much was the mean temperature below 33°C?

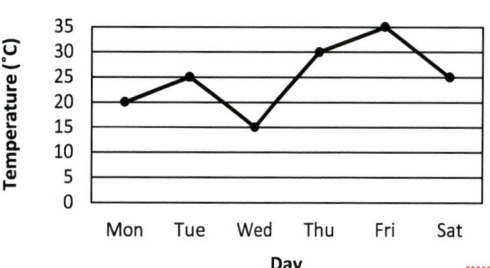

.... °C

1. A dataset consists of four numbers. The mode of the dataset is 5, the largest number is 17 and the range is 20. What is the mean of the dataset?

   ....

2. A number of children were asked if they owned a yellow, brown and purple colouring pencil. The results are shown in the Venn diagram. 29 children owned a brown colouring pencil. What fraction of children owned either a yellow pencil or a purple pencil, but not both?

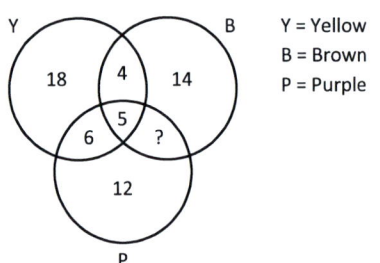

Y = Yellow
B = Brown
P = Purple

   ....

3. A car makes five journeys and uses the amount of petrol shown on the gauge. What was the average amount of petrol used per journey in millilitres? Round your final answer to the nearest thousand millilitres.

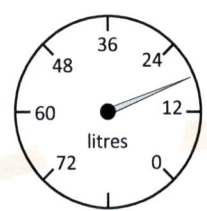

   .... ml

4. The sum of five numbers is one hundred and fifty-seven. The median number is thirty, the mode is twenty-five (which occurs twice) and the largest number is forty-two. What is the range of the five numbers?

   ....

5. Trevor took a taxi which charges the rate shown in the chart. Trevor travelled in the taxi for 2.5 miles. He paid the taxi driver's fare along with a tip of 22% of the cost of the fare. How much money did Trevor give the taxi driver in total?

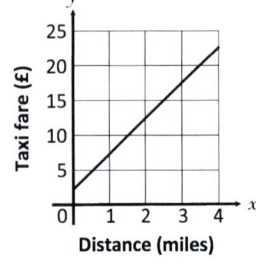

   £ ....

6. Three values in a dataset sum to 3.48. The ratio of the smallest value to the median to the largest value is 2:2:4. What is the mode value?

   ....

7. 432 people were asked what their favourite vegetable was. The results are shown on the pie chart. How many more people chose carrots than cabbage as their favourite vegetable?

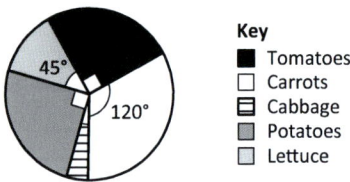

Key
■ Tomatoes
☐ Carrots
⊟ Cabbage
▨ Potatoes
▧ Lettuce

   ....

8. The chart shows temperatures over a set of weekdays. On what day was the temperature 8°C below $(3^3 - \sqrt{64} - 1^{10})$°C?

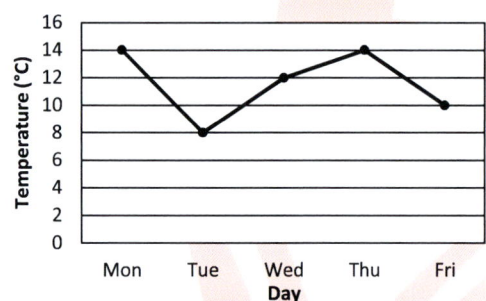

   ....

Using the table below, answer questions 9 to 13.

	Marks					
Boys	6	8	4	9	1	5
Girls	5	3	10	8	9	4

9. What is the average score for the boys?

   ....

10. What is the average score for the class?

    ....

11. What is the range?

    ....

12. What is the median mark?

    ....

13. What fraction of students scored above average?

    ....

14. Five numbers are shown below. What is the product of the mean, range and mode values?

   5   6   7   1   6

    ....

15. The lengths of six stones are shown in the chart. There are seven stones in total and the average length is 600 millimetres. What is the length of stone five in metres?

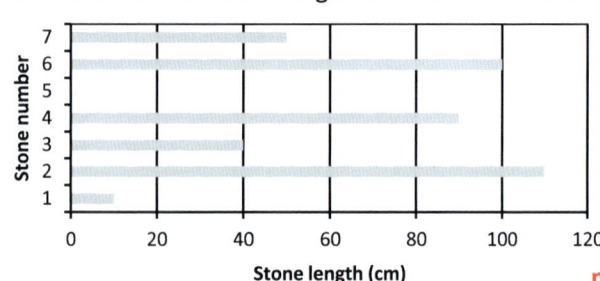

   .... m

Chapter 8

Measures and Reading Scales

1. A small pen measures 8cm in length. What is this in millimetres?

.... mm

2. What is the reading on the scales below in grams?

.... g

3. There is 2,000ml of water in a jug. What is this in litres?

.... l

4. Rima is 16cm shorter than Matt. How tall is Rima in metres? *(Diagram not to scale)*

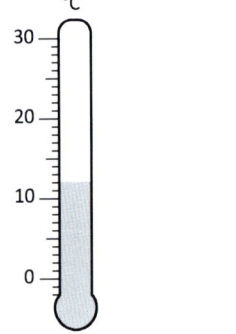

1.21m   ?

Matt   Rima

.... m

5. How many full half-pint glasses can hold the equivalent of two gallons of water? (Hint: 1 gallon = 8 pints).

....

6. Yousef walks for 2 miles. He then catches a train which takes him 10km. Approximately, how many miles did he travel in total? (Hint: 1 mile ≈ 2km).

.... miles

7. What temperature is shown on the thermometer below?

°C

30
20
10
0

.... °C

8. How many millilitres of liquid are in the container below?

1.5
1.0
0.5
litres

.... ml

9. A map is produced to a scale of 1:200. What distance in metres would be represented by 5cm on the map?

.... m

10. What is the reading represented by the arrow on the ruler below?

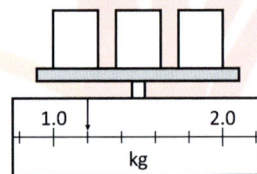

4   5

cm

.... cm

11. Salana's plan of her house extension is drawn to a scale of 1cm to 3m. The main room is 10.5m long. How long is the room in the drawing?

.... cm

12. How many grams short of 2kg is the weight shown on the scale below?

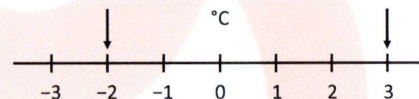

1.0   2.0

kg

.... g

13. What is the difference in temperature between the two measurements represented by the arrows on the scale below?

°C

−3 −2 −1 0 1 2 3

.... °C

14. How many 50ml glasses can be filled by using up all of the water in the jug below?

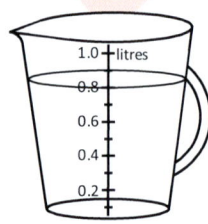

1.0 ─ litres
0.8
0.6
0.4
0.2

....

15. Which of these is the largest value? Circle your answer.

19mm   2.2cm   0.09m   6.5mm   6cm   145mm

Chapter 8: Measures and Reading Scales - Intermediate

1. What is the difference between 2500cm and 0.005km in metres?

   .... **m**

2. What is the sum of the weights of parcels 1 and 2 below in kilograms?

   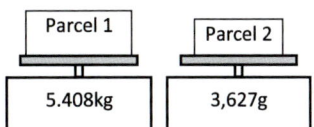

   .... **kg**

3. Nikhil has a number of £1 coins in his pocket weighing a total of 4 ounces. How much money does he have in his pocket if six £1 coins weigh approximately 2 ounces?

   £ ...... **.** ......

4. Beakers A and B below each have a capacity of 1.5 litres. What is the average amount of liquid in the two beakers in millilitres?

   (Diagram not to scale)

   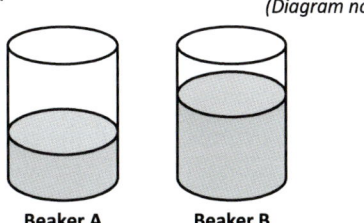

   Beaker A   **Beaker B**
   $^1/_5$ full   60% full

   .... **ml**

5. Catherine is 6 foot 2 inches tall. How many inches is this short of 90 inches? (Hint: 1 foot = 12 inches).

   .... **inches**

6. Pauline has 10.4€ in her bag. If £1 = 1.3€, how many pounds has Pauline got?

   £ ...... **.** ......

7. What is the difference between the readings represented by the arrows on the scale below?

   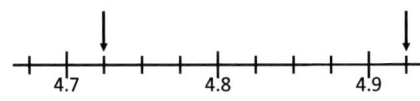

   ....

8. How many °C above minus 28°C is the temperature shown on the thermometer?

   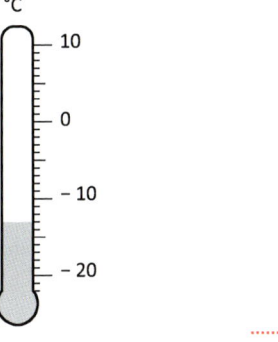

   .... **°C**

9. Damian placed some apples on the scale at his local shop as shown below. How much did the apples cost if the price was 54p per kilogram?

   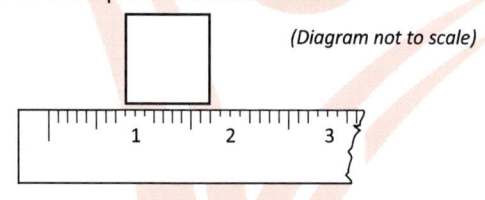

   £ ...... **.** ......

10. A map is produced to a scale of 1:1800. What distance on the map in centimetres would represent 360m in reality?

    .... **cm**

11. A square is shown below along with a ruler. What is the perimeter of the square in centimetres?

    (Diagram not to scale)

    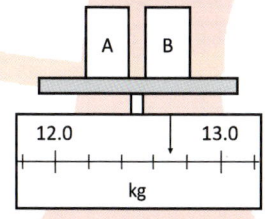

    .... **cm**

12. Two identical objects, A and B, are shown on the scales below. How much does object A weigh in grams?

    .... **g**

13. Approximately, how many more pints of liquid does the tank require to be filled to its 1.5 litre capacity? (Hint: 1 pint ≈ 500 millilitres).

    1.5
    1.0
    0.5
    litres

    .... **pints**

14. Object 1 weighs 2,850g. Object 2 weighs 80% of object 1. What is the combined weight of both objects in kilograms?

    .... **kg**

15. Luiz draws a scaled drawing of a wall. The scale is 1:260. If the full length of the wall in the drawing is 3.5cm, what is the length of half the wall in reality, in metres?

    .... **m**

1. What weight in grams would X need to be in order for the scales to achieve balance?

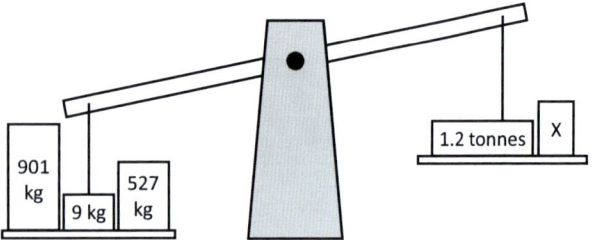

.... **g**

2. The line chart below shows the distance travelled during a car journey. How many yards had the car travelled after 1 and $^2/_3$ hours?
(Hint: 1 mile = 1,760 yards).

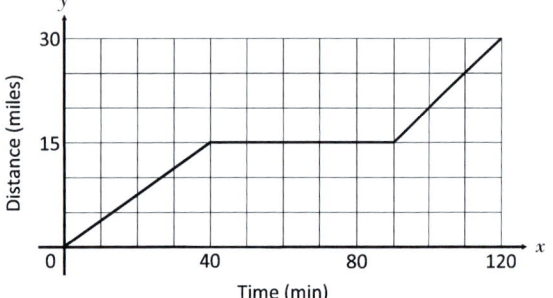

.... **yards**

3. Jude has a 2 litre container of water that is filled 78% to capacity. The container has a leak causing 50 millilitres of water to be lost every 60 seconds. How many litres of water will be left in the container after 10 minutes?

.... **l**

4. Niki draws a scaled drawing of a square field. The scale is 1:30000. What is the perimeter of the field in metres if the length of one side of the field in the drawing is √81 millimetres?

.... **m**

5. The length of a rectangle is twice its width. If the rectangle is 24cm long, what is its area in millimetres?

.... **mm²**

6. A can holds 250ml of water and costs 55 pence. A bottle holds 2 litres of water and costs £1.10. Anne-Marie buys 12 cans and four bottles. What was the average price she paid per litre of water?

.... **£ .**

7. What is the outcome from summing 12.346cm, 148mm and $1^3/_5$ cm . Present the result in cm to two decimal places?

.... **cm**

8. How many kilometres are there in 2,000cm?

.... **km**

9. Approximately, how many jugs containing the amount of liquid below would it take to fill an empty 0.9 gallon container? Hint: 1 gallon ≈ 4 litres.

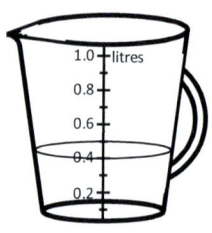

....

10. Guwon throws his javelin a distance of 90 metres and Songyo throws his a distance of 3,240 inches. Approximately, how much further did Guwon throw the javelin than Songyo in metres? (Hint: 1 inch ≈ 2.5cm).

.... **m**

11. The diameter of a five pence coin is 18mm. How many coins would fit across a length of 1.75m?

....

12. Three identical wooden sticks have a combined weight of 1 stone and 6 pounds. What is the combined weight of 18 identical wooden sticks in ounces?
Hint: 1 stone = 14 pounds and 1 pound = 16 ounces.

.... **ounces**

13. The diagram below shows three objects labelled X, Y and Z on a set of scales. Object X weighs the same as object Z, but object Y is three times the weight of object X. How much does object Z weigh in grams?

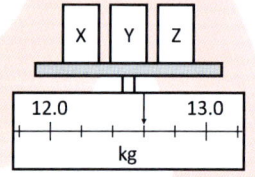

.... **g**

14. Steve drives from Torr to each of the five towns in turn on the map and back again. Approximately, how far did he travel in miles if 1 mile ≈ 2km?

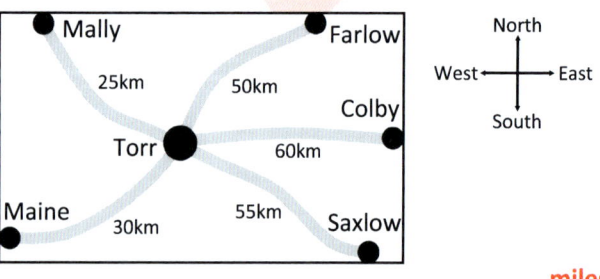

.... **miles**

15. Approximately, what is 0.029 tonnes in ounces if 1 ounce ≈ 25 grams?

.... **ounces**

Chapter 9

Dates, Times and Timetables

1. How many days does the month of June consist of?

....

2. If today is Thursday 10th December, what day of the week is 20th December?

....

3. Priti has exams coming up on the 24th March and 30th March. How many days are there between her exams?

....

4. Use the partial calendar below to determine the date of the fifth Tuesday in April.

APRIL						
Su	M	T	W	Th	F	Sa
			1	2	3	4	5
6	7	8	9	10	11	
13	14	15				

....

5. A magazine is published weekly on a Monday. If today is Tuesday 4th August, how many more magazines will be published in the remainder of August?

....

6. For how many hours does the "pm" part of each day last?

.... **hr**

7. How many seconds are in 6 minutes?

.... **sec**

8. The clock face below shows the time one morning. What is the time in 12-hour clock format?

....

9. The time now is 11.45pm. What was the time 55 minutes ago in 12-hour clock format?

....

10. What is quarter past nine in the evening in 24-hour clock format?

....

11. What is 00:18 in 12-hour clock format?

.... **:**

12. A train leaves Bournemouth station at 11:59 and calls at the following stations on its way to Waterloo. How many minutes did the train take to travel to Woking?

Station	Arrival Time
Brockenhurst	12:14
Southampton	12:31
Winchester	12:47
Woking	13:19
Waterloo	13:49

.... **min**

13. The timetables for boats A, B and C travelling from Westminster to Greenwich are shown below. If all three boats complete their journey in the same amount of time, at what time will boat C arrive at Greenwich? Express your answer in 24-hour clock format.

	Boat A	Boat B	Boat C
Westminster	10:45	11:15	11:45
London Eye	10:55	11:25	11:55
Tower of London	11:25	11:55	12:25
Greenwich	11:55	12:25	?

.... **:**

14. The table below shows departure times of a train travelling from Sheffield to Oxford. A ticket officer gets on the train at Derby and stays on until the train reaches Oxford. For how many minutes was the ticket officer on board the train?

Station	Departure Times
Sheffield	11:24
Derby	11:53
Birmingham New Street	12:33
Leamington Spa	13:00
Banbury	13:19
Oxford	13:43

.... **min**

15. Alex leaves town A at 19:21 and walks to town B. He arrives at town B at 19:47. He waits at town B for 20 minutes. He then walks back to town A. The return walk between the towns takes him the same time as the walk he made earlier. At what time, in 24-hour clock format, does Alex return to town A?

.... **:**

1. How many days are there in total in October, November and December?

   ....

2. If today is Monday 1st June, what fraction of the days in this month will be Saturdays or Sundays?

   ....

3. Jia went on holiday on Saturday 27th July and returned the following month on the 6th. On what day of the week did Jia return?

   ....

4. Mike was issued with the following train ticket for a journey he took exactly 120 hours ago. What is the date now?

TRAIN TICKET
Ticket Number: 124
From: Stockbridge   To: Ferndown
Valid at 13:06 on 29th April

   ....

5. Panos was born on 29th February in the year 1992. It is now 29th February 2016 and Panos is celebrating his birthday. How many times has 29th February occurred between his birth and now, inclusive of both events?

   ....

6. Today, Clock A shows a time of 5.51am and zero seconds. Clock B shows a time of 5.53am and zero seconds. Clock B gains 20 seconds every day, while clock A does not gain or lose any time. How many days ago did both clocks show exactly the same time?

   ....

7. What is the difference in minutes between 21:14 and 11.37pm on the same day?

   .... min

8. Stella is going to the theatre one evening. She leaves home at 18:30 and each part of the evening along with its duration is shown below. What time, in 24-hour clock format, does the second half of the performance start?

Section	Duration (minutes)
Travel to theatre	70
First Half	60
Interval	20
Second Half	50
Travel Home	45

   .... :

9. In two-thirds of an hour it will be quarter to five in the afternoon. What time, in 12-hour clock format, is it now?

   ....

10. John's train left Bristol 4 minutes late, at 10:02. It arrived in Reading 120 seconds early, at 11:09. How long would the journey have taken if the train had left and arrived on time?

    .... min

11. The clock on the left shows a time this morning, while the clock on the right shows the time this afternoon. How many full hours have passed since the time this morning?

    .... hr

12. Look at the train timetable below. Pierre left Ealing Broadway station on the 12:33 train to spend some time in Bath. He left Bath at 19:20 by bus to travel on to a nearby town. For how long was Pierre actually in Bath?

	Train 1	Train 2	Train 3	Train 4
Paddington	12:15	12:18	12:25	12:40
Ealing Broadway	12:23	12:27	12:33	12:48
Maidenhead	13:05	13:10	13:26	13:41
Reading	13:26	13:43	13:56	14:11
Bath	14:28	14:57	15:29	15:44

    .... min

13. The diagram below shows a bus timetable from Peacehaven to Lewes. 34 minutes into its journey, what stop will the bus call at next?

Stop	Time
Peacehaven	07:17
Newhaven	07:34
Piddinghoc	07:48
Rodmell	07:53
Southover	08:01
Lewes	08:09

    ....

14. At which station below was the train stationary for the second longest amount of time?

Station	Arrival	Departure
Allex	19:01	19:02
Blex	19:21	19:23
Cloud	19:27	19:35
Drez	19:58	20:04
Epex	20:30	20:33

15. How many hours are there in 3.75 days?

    .... hr

Chapter 9: Dates, Times and Timetables - Advanced

1. What is the difference between the sum of the number of days in the odd numbered months (i.e. January, March, May etc.), and the sum of the number of days in the even numbered months (i.e. February, April, June etc.)? Assume it is not a leap year.

   ....

2. How many minutes later is 02.34am on Sunday morning than 22:49 on Saturday?

   .... **min**

3. From the table below, give the time that is closest to the 'pm' time shown on the clock? Circle your answer.

Times
20:03
11.20pm
218 minutes before midnight
8.8 hours after noon
900 seconds short of 8.57pm

4. Heather leaves home at 9.00am one morning and completes the tasks below in order without a break. At what time, in 12-hour clock format, does she complete the five tasks?

Task	Duration
Walk to town	35 minutes
Have breakfast	42 minutes
Shop	1.9 hours
Have a coffee	420 seconds
Bus ride home	15 minutes

   ....

5. Mrs Patel went on a business trip on Thursday 28th June. She returned home on 2nd August. On which day of the week did Mrs Patel return home?

   ....

6. The table below shows the times at which 5 trains called at stations between Manchester and Stoke-on-Trent. Trains 2, 3 and 4 did not call at all the stations. Which train was the third fastest to complete its journey?

	Train 1	Train 2	Train 3	Train 4	Train 5
Manchester	08:53	10:17	11:35	12:17	13:26
Stockport	09:01	10:26	11:43	12:25	13:39
Macclesfield	09:23	10:38	11:58	12:38	14:03
Congleton	09:31	---	---	12:49	14:10
Kidsgrove	09:37	---	---	---	14:16
Stoke-on-Trent	09:49	11:00	12:23	13:03	14:33

   ....

7. What percentage of months with a name beginning with a J or D have 31 days?

   .... **%**

8. A runner completes the 100 metres sprint in 10.5 seconds, 11.8 seconds, 10.0 seconds, 12.5 seconds, 11.2 seconds and 15.8 seconds. For every time the runner completes the distance in less than $\sqrt{121}$ seconds he receives £4. For every time he completes the distance in less than $(2^4 - 2^0)$ seconds he receives £3. For all other times he receives nothing. How much did he receive from his times above?

   £ .... **.** ......

9. How many hours short of 100 hours is the number of hours in $3\,^7/_8$ days?

   .... **hr**

10. Aga spent exactly one sixth of November completing her school project. If she completed the project on the 16th of that month, what date did she start the project?

    ....

11. Zoltan worked the following hours last week. He took one hour for lunch each day. How many hours did he work in the week?

Day	Start time	End time
Mon	09:15	17:50
Tue	08:50	17:10
Wed	08:00	16:05
Thu	09:30	16:00
Fri	09:00	16:00

    .... **hr**

12. How many full weeks are in two full non leap years?

    ....

13. The television coverage for a football match begins at 14:35. The first and second half last 45 minutes each and 15 minutes was given for half-time. What time, in 24-hour clock format, is a third of the way through the second half?

    .... **:**

14. If a week starts on Sunday 4th at 00:00, what date and time (12-hour clock format) is exactly halfway through the week?

    ....

15. Kriti lives at Fulford and took the 10:37 bus to Barlby. Anita lives in Escrick and left on the 11:34 bus to Barlby to meet her friend Kriti for lunch. How long did Kriti have to wait at the Barlby bus stop for Anita to arrive?

	Bus A	Bus B	Bus C
York	10:30	11:10	11:35
Fulford	10:37	11:19	11:44
Escrick	10:49	11:34	11:59
Riccall	10:55	11:40	12:05
Barlby	11:01	11:46	12:11
Selby	11:15	12:00	12:25

    .... **min**

FIRST PAST THE POST®

Chapter 10

Lines, Angles and Bearings

1. Which line below is a vertical line? Circle your answer.

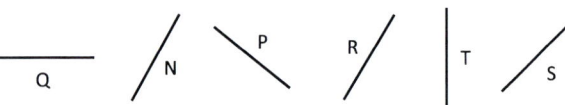

2. What is the length of the line that is perpendicular to line D below?

(Diagram not to scale)

.... **cm**

3. What do the exterior angles in a hexagon sum to?

.... °

4. What do the interior angles in a triangle sum to?

.... °

5. What is the size of angle q?

(Diagram not to scale)

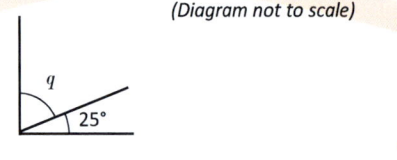

.... °

6. What is the name for an angle which is greater than 180°?

....

7. The circle below has been cut into 12 equal sectors. What is the size of angle x?

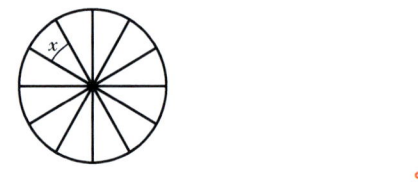

.... °

8. What is the size of angle x in the diagram below?

(Diagram not to scale)

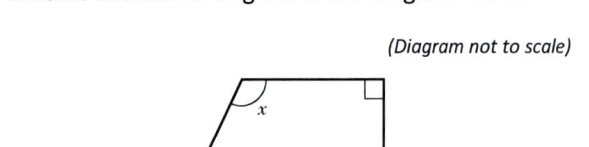

.... °

9. What is the size of angle y in the diagram below?

(Diagram not to scale)

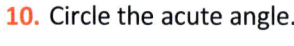

.... °

10. Circle the acute angle.

   93°   90°   190°   45°   180°   478°

11. What is the size of angle c in the regular polygon below?

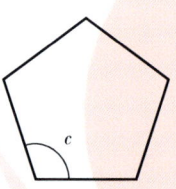

.... °

12. What is the opposite direction of south?

....

13. On a compass, which two directions are at right angles to south?

....

14. In which diagram below (A to E), is the post box west of the building?

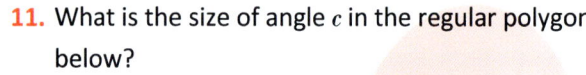

....

15. Which corner on the square below is north-west of corner S?

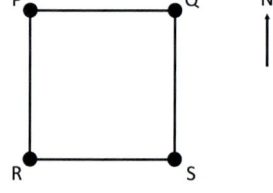

....

1. What is the difference between an angle in an equilateral triangle and the smaller angle between two perpendicular lines?

.... °

2. What is the average length of all the lines below that are parallel?

(Diagram not to scale)

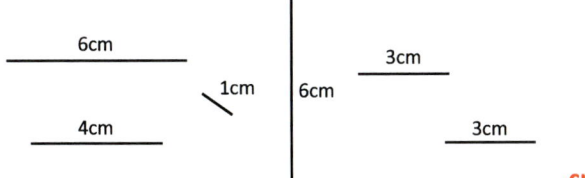

.... **cm**

3. The length of the shorter diagonal on the rhombus below is 35% the length of the longest diagonal. What is the length of the shortest diagonal?

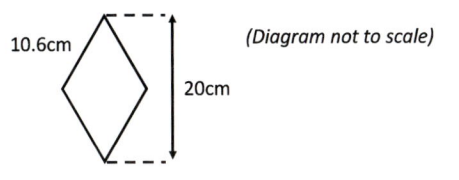

(Diagram not to scale)

.... **cm**

4. 35° and 78° are two angles in a triangle. What type of triangle is this?

....

5. What angle is $^3/_8$ of a right angle?

.... °

6. What is the size of angle R in the diagram below?

(Diagram not to scale)

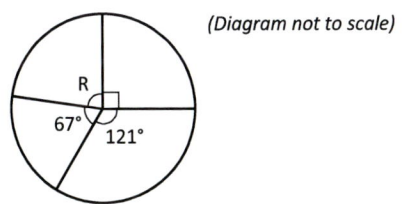

.... °

7. What is the size of angle X in the kite below?

(Diagram not to scale)

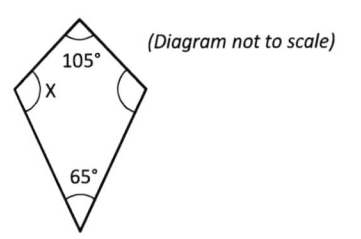

.... °

8. If the largest angle in a triangle is 130°, what is the maximum size that the second largest angle could be, assuming angles can only be measured in whole numbers?

.... °

9. What is the size of angle Y in the parallelogram below?

(Diagram not to scale)

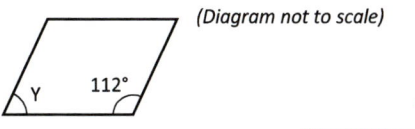

.... °

10. If the hour hand on a clock face turns through 120° clockwise from 6.00pm, what will the new time be in 12-hour clock format?

....

11. What is the sum of angles C and D in the regular octagon below?

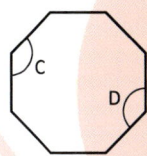

.... °

12. On a compass, how many degrees anticlockwise is the turn from south-west to east?

.... °

13. Anna is facing west and turns through 315° clockwise. In what direction is Anna now facing?

....

14. Tasos is standing on the grey shaded square on the grid below. In what direction from him is the square with the largest prime number on the grid?

1	2	3	4	5
6	7	8	9	10
11	12	13	14	15
16		18	19	20
21	22	23	24	25

N ↑

....

15. If the school is directly north of Billy and the shop is west of him, in what direction is the post office from him?

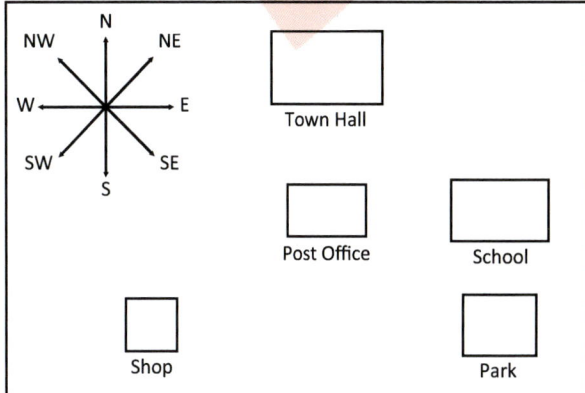

....

1. What is the smallest possible whole number-sized angle in an acute-angle triangle?

..............................°

2. Rohit records the numbers of the sides that are perpendicular to side 5 below. He sums them and squares the result. How much less than 113.8 is the result?

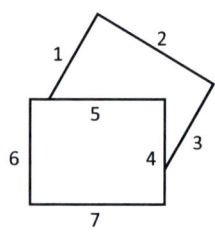

....

3. What is the value of angle A shown on the clock face below?

..............................°

4. The angles in a triangle are in the ratio 2:10:3. What is the size of the smallest angle?

..............................°

5. The perimeter of a regular octagon with two vertical sides is 132cm. How much more than 650mm is the sum of all its horizontal and vertical side lengths?

..............................**mm**

6. What is the result of taking angle *b* away from *a*?

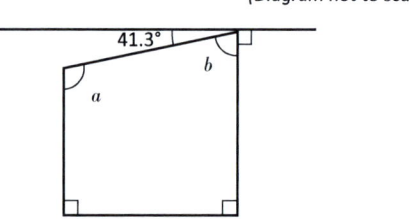

(Diagram not to scale)

..............................°

7. The smallest angle in a triangle is *q*. The next smallest angle is twice the angle *q*. The largest angle is five times the value of *q*. What is the size of the largest angle?

..............................°

8. What is the sum of all the reflex angles below?

90°   91.32°   341.72°   181.97°   0.89°

219.56°   2.73°

..............................°

9. What is $^3/_4$ of three right-angles?

..............................°

10. What is the size of angle Q below?

(Diagram not to scale)

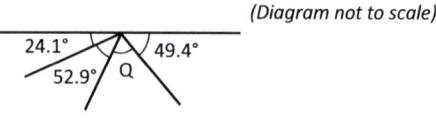

..............................°

11. Which of these instructions should be followed to travel along the shaded path from the START square to the FINISH square?

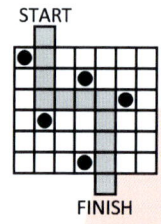

a) Forward 3, Turn right 90°, Forward 3, Turn Left 90°, Forward 4.

b) Forward 2, Turn left 90°, Forward 4, Turn right 90°, Forward 3.

c) Forward 3, Turn left 90°, Forward 3, Turn right 90°, Forward 4.

d) Forward 4, Turn right 90°, Forward 2, Turn left 90°, Forward 5.

e) Forward 3, Turn left 90°, Forward 4, Turn right 90°, Forward 3.

....

12. Vera is standing at the centre of a large clock face. She is facing north and looking at the number 7. What number on the clock face is directly west of her?

....

13. What is the size of angle X in the regular hexagon below?

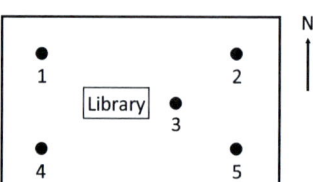

..............................°

14. Each of the following 5 people are at one of the numbered points on the grid below. Albert is north of Marta. Jess is east of Marta and south of Alan. Sophie is the only other person on the diagram. What direction is Sophie from the Library?

....

15. How many degrees is the clockwise turn from south-west to north-west?

..............................°

FIRST PAST THE POST®

Chapter 11

2D Shapes, Perimeter, Area and Symmetry

1. What is the name of the polygon below?

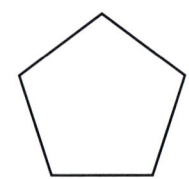

....

2. What is the name of a triangle in which all three sides are equal in length?

....

3. How many pairs of parallel sides does a parallelogram have?

....

4. A rectangle is shown below. What is the length of Y?

(Diagram not to scale)

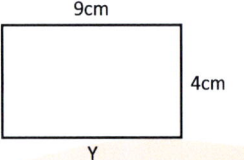

.... **cm**

5. The diameter of a circle is 10cm. What is the length of its radius?

.... **cm**

6. How many sides of equal length does a rhombus have?

....

7. What is the name of a polygon with nine sides?

....

8. What is the perimeter of the rectangular garden below?

(Diagram not to scale)

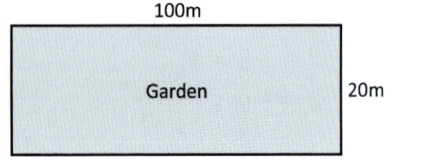

.... **m**

9. A square has an area of 49m². What is the perimeter of the square?

.... **m**

10. By how many cm² is the area of the square larger than the area of the rectangle below?

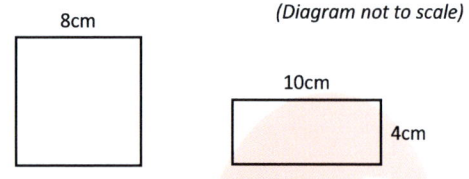

(Diagram not to scale)

.... **cm²**

11. Rectangle R is shown below. If each square that makes up the rectangle has an area of 11mm², what is the area of R?

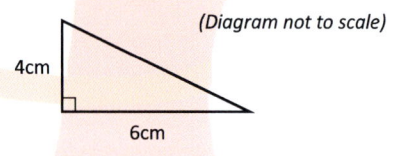

.... **mm²**

12. What is the area of the triangle below?

(Diagram not to scale)

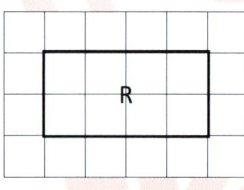

.... **cm²**

13. How many lines of symmetry does a square have?

....

14. What is the order of rotational symmetry for the regular polygon below?

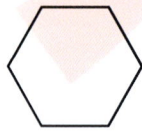

....

15. Which one of shapes 1 to 4 below, is shown with an incorrect line of symmetry?

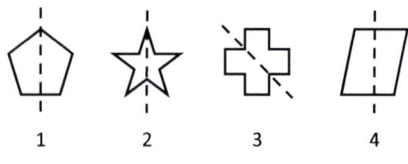

....

1. What is the total number of sides in the shapes below?

....

2. A symmetrical shape has two equal interior obtuse angles and two equal interior acute angles along with one pair of parallel sides and one line of symmetry. What is the shape?

....

3. How many of the following seven terms are names of parts of a circle?

sector   arc   diameter   corner

circumference   polygon   semicircle

....

4. A circle inside a square is shown below. The sum of the length of two sides on the square is 50cm. What is the radius of the circle?

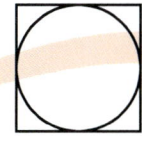

.... cm

5. What percentage of the shapes below are polygons with at least one pair of perpendicular sides?

.... %

6. How many of the following five shapes are regular quadrilaterals?

square   oblong   equilateral triangle   kite   rhombus

....

7. What is the name of the polygon whose interior angles sum to 720°?

....

8. The perimeter of a regular octagon is 16,800m. What is the length of one side in kilometres?

.... km

9. What is the expression for the perimeter of the square below?

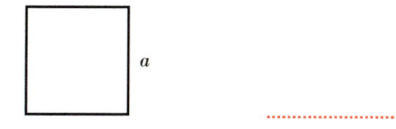

....

10. What is the perimeter of the triangle below?

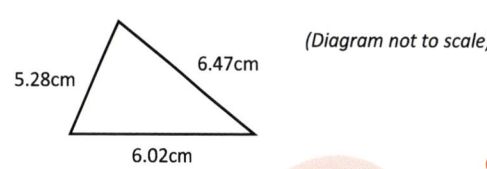

(Diagram not to scale)

.... cm

11. A shape is shown on the grid below. If each square on the grid has an area of 13.5cm^2, what is the area of the shape?

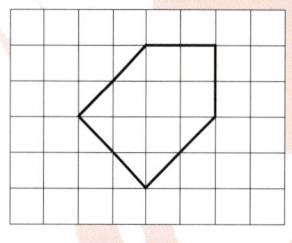

.... cm^2

12. The area of the rectangle below is 36cm^2. What is the length of Y in millimetres?

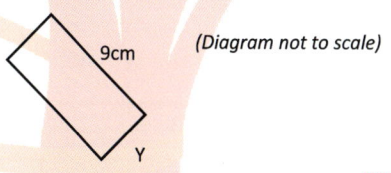

(Diagram not to scale)

.... mm

13. How many of the following capital letters have at least one line of symmetry?

E Y H Q M T V

....

14. Part of a regular shape is shown below along with two lines of symmetry. What is the order of rotational symmetry of the full shape?

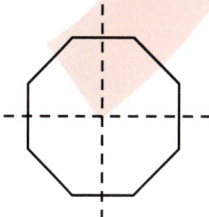

....

15. How many lines of symmetry do all the five shapes below have in total?

2 squares   1 kite   1 rectangle   1 parallelogram

43

1. What is the perimeter of the shape below in centimetres?

   (Diagram not to scale)

   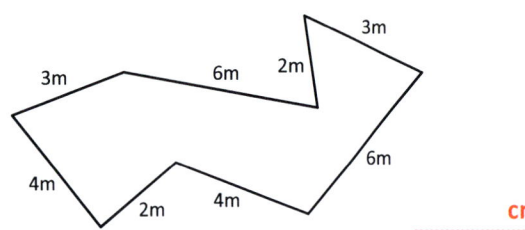

   _____ **cm**

2. The largest side of a rectangle is 18.5cm. Could its area be 350cm^2?

   _____

3. Two concentric circles are shown below. The diameter of the smaller circle is $^3/_7$ the size of the diameter of the larger circle. If the diameter of the larger circle is 1.4m, what is the radius of the smaller circle in centimetres?

   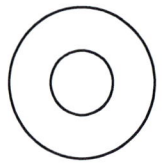

   _____ **cm**

4. What percentage of the capital letters below have both line symmetry and rotational symmetry?

   D   Y   U   H   A   F   X   T

   _____ **%**

5. The perimeter of the symmetrical trapezium below is 52cm. What is its area?

   (Diagram not to scale)

   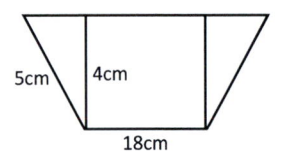

   _____ **cm^2**

6. A 2D shape has 2 pairs of adjacent equal sides, 1 pair of equal angles, a line symmetry of 1, and no rotational symmetry. What shape is this describing?

   _____

7. How many pairs of parallel sides are in all the 2D shapes shown below?

   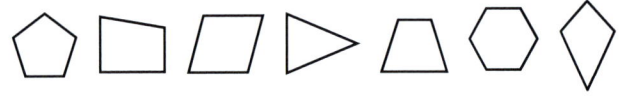

   _____

8. What is the area of the shape below to the nearest 10m^2?

   (Diagram not to scale)

   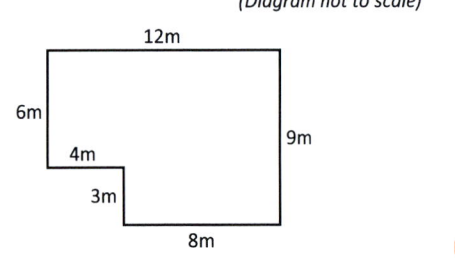

   _____ **m^2**

9. What is the simplified expression for the perimeter of the shape below?

   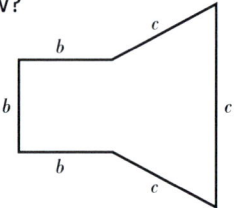

   _____

10. The diagram below shows a shape and two of its lines of symmetry. All sides of the shape are equal. How many lines of symmetry does the shape have in total?

    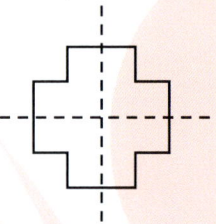

    _____

11. Two identical circles inside a rectangle are shown below. If the radius of each circle is 17mm, what is the perimeter of the rectangle in centimetres?

    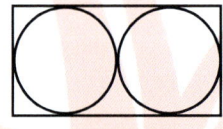

    _____ **cm**

12. A square, parallelogram, regular heptagon and an obtuse-angled triangle are on a table. Which two statements below are false? Circle your answers.

    a) The two smallest angles in the triangle must both be less than 90°.
    b) The triangle is the only irregular shape of the four.
    c) Only one of the four shapes has a side that is perpendicular to another side.
    d) All four shapes are polygons.
    e) Three of the four shapes are quadrilaterals.

13. What is the difference in areas between the shape with the largest area and the shape with the smallest area?

    (Diagram not to scale)

    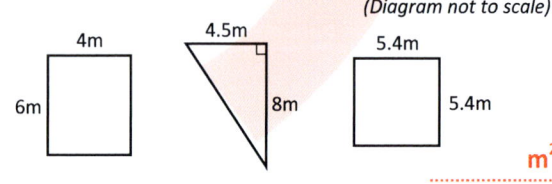

    _____ **m^2**

14. A tailor has 113.8cm^2 of material. How many whole squares with a perimeter of 16cm could he cut from this material?

    _____

15. The area of a right-angled triangle is 24.75cm^2. The length of its horizontal base is 3cm. What is its height?

    _____ **cm**

FIRST PAST THE POST®

Chapter 12

3D Shapes and Volume

1. What is the name of the 3D shape below?

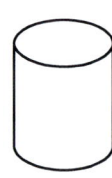

2. How many edges does the shape below have?

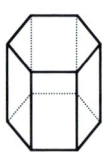

3. What is the name of the 3D shape below?

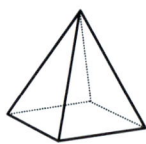

4. How many vertices does a cuboid have?

5. How many faces does a pentagonal prism have?

6. What 3D shape is formed when the net below is folded up?

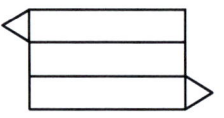

7. The net below forms a cube when folded up. Is it a closed or open cube?

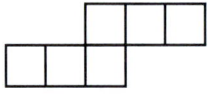

8. What 3D shape is formed when the net below is folded up?

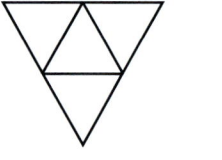

9. A large fish tank is 8 metres in length, 3 metres in breadth and 5 metres in height. What is its volume?

.... m^3

10. The volume of a cube is 27cm^3. What is the length of one of its edges?

.... cm

11. What is the volume of the block below?

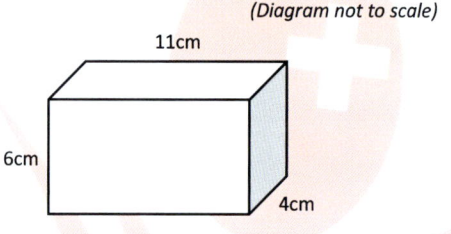

(Diagram not to scale)

11cm

6cm

4cm

.... cm^3

12. Find the volume of the cuboid below, given that each small cube is 2cm^3 in volume.

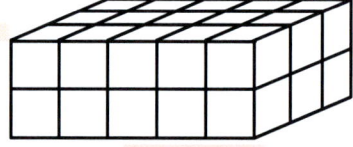

.... cm^3

13. The volume of a cube is 64cm^3. How many smaller cubes of volume 8cm^3 could fit inside the larger cube?

14. The dimensions of two cuboids are shown below. Which cuboid has the smaller volume?
a) length 5cm, breadth 10cm, height 8cm
b) length 6cm, breadth 11cm, height 6cm

15. Cube A has a volume of 40m^3. The volume of cube B is three-quarters the volume of cube A. What is the combined volume of both cubes?

.... m^3

1. How many pairs of parallel faces does a cube have?

....

2. What is the difference between the number of edges in a cuboid and a square-based pyramid?

....

3. What is the combined number of faces of the three shapes below?

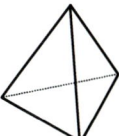  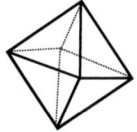

....

4. Which 3D shape has twice as many vertices as a triangular prism?

....

5. Vanashri has 26 identical hemispheres. She glues each one to another one to form spheres. A box can hold four spheres. How many boxes can be completely filled?

....

6. The net below forms a closed box. What is the perimeter of the smallest face of the box?

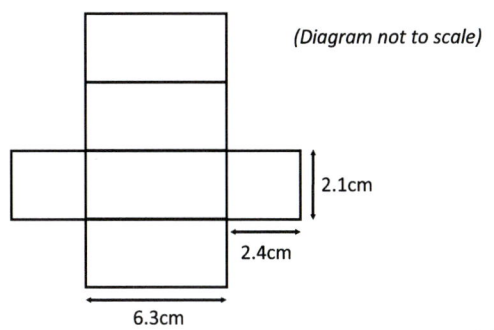

(Diagram not to scale)

2.1cm

2.4cm

6.3cm

.... **cm**

7. Alina wants to produce a net for a regular octagonal prism. She has two identical rectangles and two identical octagons. How many more identical rectangles will she need to complete the net?

....

8. The volume of a cuboid is 120m³. Its length is 6m and its height is 10m. What is its breadth?

.... **m**

9. What is the volume of a cuboid room with length 12m, breadth 5m and height 300cm?

.... **m³**

10. The area of a face of a cube is 25cm². What is the volume of the cube?

.... **cm³**

11. What is the volume of the triangular shaped wedge below?

(Diagram not to scale)

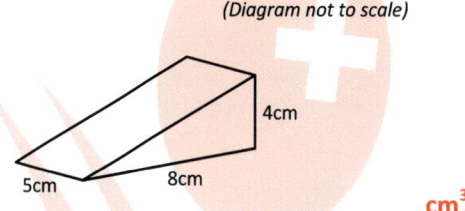

4cm

5cm   8cm

.... **cm³**

12. The net below forms a cube when folded up. Which face is parallel to the base when the cube is formed?

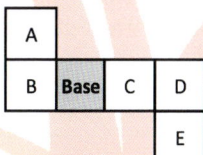

....

13. Given that the volume of each small cube is 12.5cm³, what is the volume of the cuboid below?

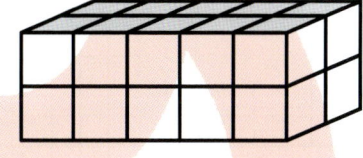

.... **cm³**

14. A cylindrical tin of soup is 17cm in height and the area of its circular base is 50cm². What is its volume?

.... **cm³**

15. The cuboid shown below has its dimensions expressed in Roman numerals. What is its volume?

(Diagram not to scale)

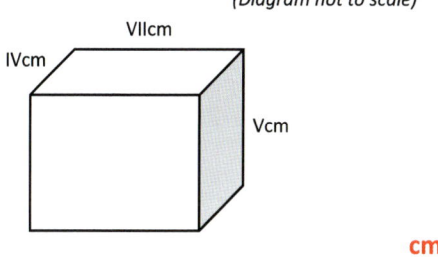

VIIcm

IVcm

Vcm

.... **cm³**

Chapter 12: 3D Shapes and Volume - Advanced

1. How many faces are in three cubes, two hexagonal prisms and one triangular prism?

....

2. How many faces in a regular octagonal prism have three or more pairs of parallel edges?

....

3. What is the total number of vertices on all the shapes below?

....

4. 347 traffic cones are placed on one side of a straight road, in a line. They each measure 30cm across at their widest point. What is the minimum length of the road?

.... m

5. How many of the shapes below do not have a prime or triangular number for their number of faces?

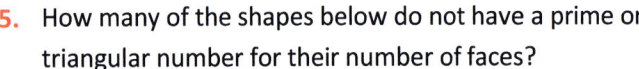
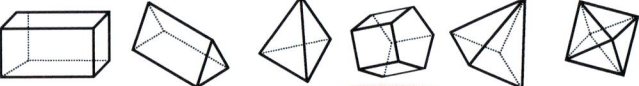

....

6. The net below is of a cuboid. The volume of the cuboid is 212cm³. What is the volume of one of the cubes which make up the cuboid?

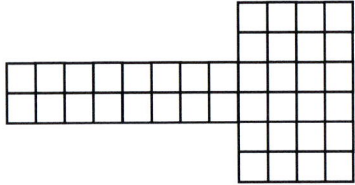

.... cm³

7. What is the volume of a cuboid with length 3.5cm, breadth 9cm and height 70mm?

.... cm³

8. What is the maximum number of marbles, with a diameter of 2cm, that could be put inside the box shown below?

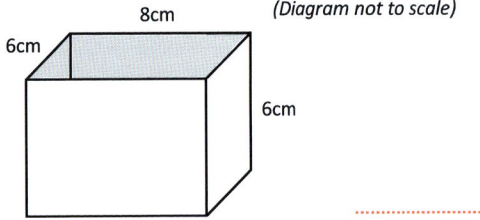

(Diagram not to scale)

8cm
6cm
6cm

....

9. What is the volume of the shape below?

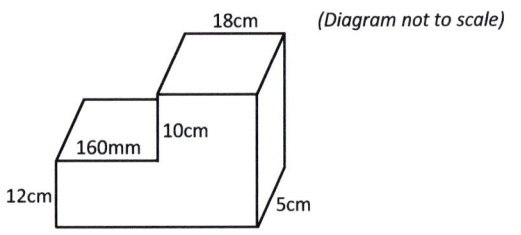

18cm *(Diagram not to scale)*
160mm
10cm
12cm
5cm

.... cm³

10. The volume of a cube is 216cm³. What is the perimeter of one of its faces?

.... cm

11. Given that each small cube is 1.08cm³, what is the volume of the large cube shown below?

.... cm³

12. The volume of a sphere is 25.8cm³. The volume of a cone is 15.7cm³. What is the combined volume of four identical spheres and five identical cones?

.... cm³

13. The volume of the container below is 2,000cm³ and the area of the circular top A is 100cm². What is the depth of water in the container?

(Diagram not to scale)

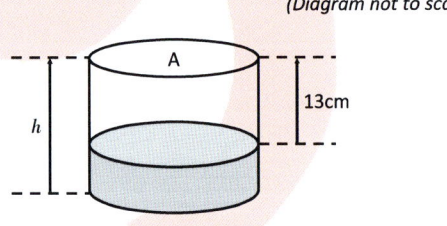

A
13cm
h

.... cm

14. The volume of a cuboid is 210cm³. Its length is 5cm and its height is 7cm. What is its breadth in millimetres?

.... mm

15. The length of a cuboid is 8cm. Its breadth is 3.5 times its length and its height is $^3/_{16}$ of its length. What is the volume of the cuboid?

.... cm³

FIRST PAST THE POST®

Chapter 13

Probability

Use the following diagram to answer the statements in questions 1 to 5 by choosing one of the five probabilities on the scale, as your answer.

Impossible	Unlikely	Even Chance	Likely	Certain

1. February will contain more than 29 days.

   ....

2. It will rain on at least one day in London during March.

   ....

3. You toss a fair coin and it lands heads up.

   ....

4. The next Prime Minister of the United Kingdom will be over 10 years of age.

   ....

5. A brand new car will break down on two consecutive days.

   ....

6. What is the probability that the spinner lands on a grey section? Give your answer as a fraction.

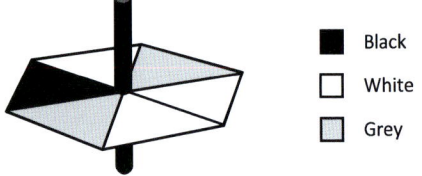

   ■ Black
   □ White
   ▨ Grey

   ....

7. Emma rolls a fair die. What is the probability the die lands face up on an even number? Give your answer as a decimal.

   ....

8. Johan selects a numbered disc at random from the bag below. What is the probability that the disc does not have a 3 on it? Give your answer as a fraction.

9. The letters below are shuffled and put in an empty box. What is the probability that the first letter drawn from the box is a 'G'? Give your answer as a decimal.

   D I G I T

   ....

10. If today is Monday, what is the probability that tomorrow is Tuesday? Give your answer as a percentage.

   .... %

11. A card is chosen at random from a standard pack of 52 playing cards. What is the probability that the card is one of those shown below? Give your answer as a fraction.

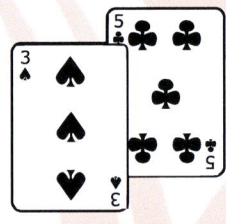

   ....

12. A bag contains four orange marbles and three blue marbles. A marble is selected at random from the bag. What is the probability that it is green in colour?

   ....

13. A book contains 10 pages. Eight of the pages have photographs on them. What is the probability that a page chosen at random has a photograph on it? Give your answer as a fraction.

   ....

14. Andrew rolls a fair die. What is the probability the die lands face up on a number greater than 2? Give your answer as a fraction.

   ....

15. A circle is chosen at random from those shown below. What is the probability that it is shaded? Give your answer as a fraction.

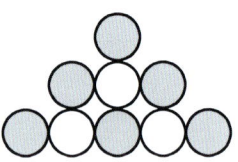

Use the following diagram to answer the statements in questions 1 to 5 by choosing one of the five probabilities on the scale as your answer.

Impossible　　Unlikely　　Even Chance　　Likely　　Certain

1. At least one leap year will occur in the next eight years.

....

2. A fair die is rolled 12 times and the number 6 is not recorded at all.

....

3. Today is Friday. Yesterday was Thursday and tomorrow is Sunday.

....

4. A month chosen at random from June, January, December and November has 31 days.

....

5. A season chosen at random from winter, spring, summer and autumn has the letter 'n' in its name.

....

6. A square is selected at random from the grid below. What is the probability that the square contains an image of a bicycle? Give your answer as a fraction.

....

7. A card is selected at random from a standard pack of 52 playing cards. What is the probability that it is a red card which is either an ace or a king? Give your answer as a fraction.

....

8. Max tosses two fair coins. What is the probability that they both land tails up? Give your answer as a decimal.

....

9. The table below shows test marks for a set of students. What is the probability that a student selected at random scored either 5 or 8 on the test? Give your answer as a fraction.

Test Marks	8	9	6	8	7	7	8	5	5

....

10. Roza selects a day of the week at random. What is the probability that it has exactly eight letters in its name? Give your answer as a fraction.

....

11. What is the probability that the spinner lands on a number which is less than or equal to 15? Give your answer as a fraction.

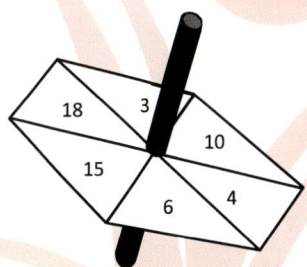

12. A fair die is rolled. What is the probability that it lands face up on an odd number greater than 1? Give your answer as a fraction.

....

13. A bag contains 15 green balls and 12 purple balls. A ball is selected at random. What is the probability that it is not purple in colour? Give your answer as a fraction.

....

14. The probability that a netball team wins a match is $^5/_6$. If a netball team plays 18 matches, how many matches would the team expect to win?

....

15. Andrea takes classes in English, maths, science, geography, history, technology, music and computing. She selects one of these subjects at random. What is the probability that it is a subject that begins with an 'm'? Give your answer as a percentage.

.... %

1. Adnan tosses two fair coins. What is the probability that exactly one coin will land tails up and the other will land heads up? Give your answer as a fraction.

   ....

2. Rhea removes the four cards shown below from a standard pack of 52 playing cards. She then selects one card at random from the cards remaining in the pack. What is the probability that it is a diamond or a queen? Give your answer as a fraction.

   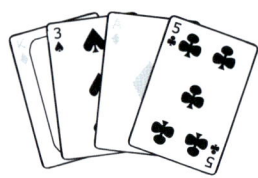

   ....

3. Anna rolls two fair dice. What is the probability that the total of the two dice is 7? Give your answer as a fraction.

   ....

4. What is the probability that the spinner lands on a grey or white section? Give your answer as a percentage.

   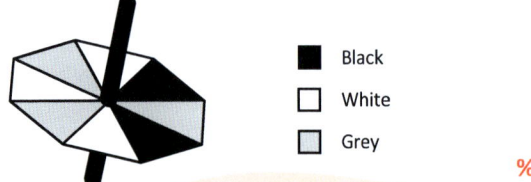

   ■ Black
   □ White
   ▨ Grey

   ....%

5. A purse contains three 10 pence coins, five 20 pence coins, eight 50 pence coins and six £1 coins. A coin is selected from the purse at random. What is the probability that it is worth at least 50 pence? Give your answer as a fraction.

   ....

6. A fair die is rolled 114 times. How many times would you expect to obtain a value of less than 3?

   ....

7. A numbered disc is selected at random from the bag below. What is the probability that it is larger than 5 but no larger than 12? Give your answer as a fraction.

   ....

8. The letters in the word below are shuffled and three are chosen at random, without replacement. What is the probability that the first letter selected is a 'C' followed by an 'A' and lastly a 'P' to spell 'CAP'? Give your answer as a fraction.

   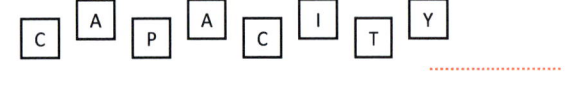

   ....

9. The probability that a team wins a game of volleyball is $^3/_{13}$ and the probability of a draw is $^1/_4$. The only other outcome is a loss for the team. What is the probability that the team loses a game? Give your answer as a fraction.

   ....

10. Hussain has two sets of balls. He selects one ball at random from each set. What is the probability that they are both shaded? Give your answer as a percentage.

    Set 1   Set 2

    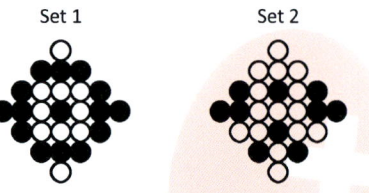

    ....%

11. The probability that a book contains zero errors is 6% and the probability that a book contains one error is 29%. There are 40 books in a set. How many of them are likely to contain fewer than two errors?

    ....

12. If the fair spinner below was spun 104 times, on how many occasions would you expect the spinner to land on a 5?

    ....

13. A card is taken at random from a standard pack of 52 playing cards. Which one of the five statements below is false?

    a) The probability of selecting a club is equal to the probability of selecting a heart.

    b) The probability of selecting a jack, queen, king or ace is unlikely.

    c) The probability of not selecting a club is likely.

    d) The probability of selecting a red 7 or 8 is $^1/_{13}$.

    e) The probability of selecting the ace of hearts is equal to the probability of selecting a black ace.

    ....

14. Which one of the five probabilities on the scale describes the chance of spinning a coin with two heads 488 times and getting 244 tails.

    Impossible   Unlikely   Even Chance   Likely   Certain

    ....

15. A fair die and fair coin are both thrown. What is the probability that the coin shows a head and the die does not show a 1 or 6? Give your answer as a fraction.

    ....

Chapter 14

Coordinates and Transformations

1. Which lettered point is at coordinates (2, 3) on the grid below?

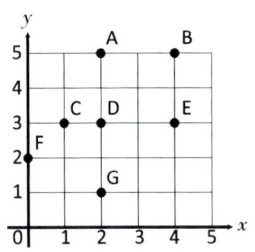

....

2. A straight line lies between coordinates (0, 1) to (0, 5). What are the coordinates of the midpoint of the line?

(,   )

3. What are the coordinates of point Q on the rectangle below?

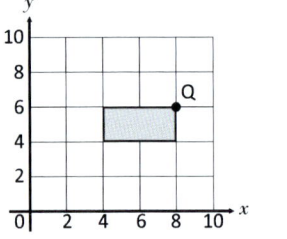

(,   )

4. The corner coordinates of a triangle are at (0, 0), (3, 0) and (0, 4). Both axes have the same scale. What is the name of this type of triangle?

....

5. What are the coordinates of the ship below?

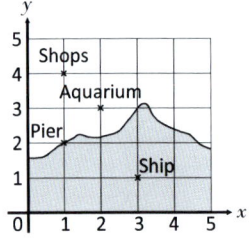

(,   )

6. Between which two coordinates does a straight line need to be drawn on the grid below to form a trapezium?

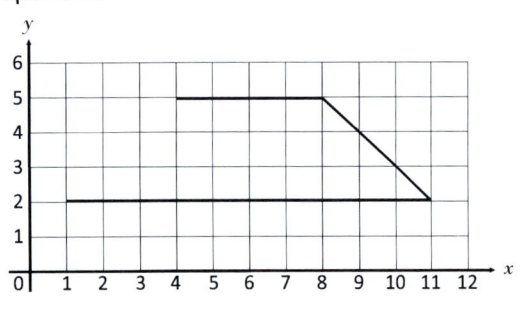

(,   ) and (,   )

7. Point V at coordinates (5, 0) is rotated 90° anticlockwise about the origin. What are the new coordinates of point V?

(,   )

8. Point A at coordinates (1, 1) is translated right by three units. What are its new coordinates?

(,   )

9. The points (3, 0), (5, 4), (3, 6) and (1, 4) are plotted on a grid and joined up in order using straight lines. What object is formed?

....

10. Point Q on the grid below is translated up three units and left one unit. What are its new coordinates?

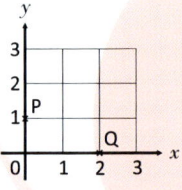

(,   )

11. The circle on the grid below is translated two units up and one unit right. What are the new coordinates for the centre of the circle?

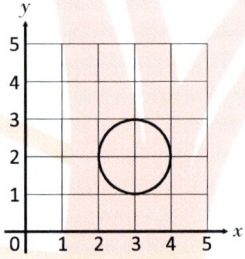

(,   )

12. Point B at coordinates (0, 2) is reflected in the line $x = 2$. What are the new coordinates of point B?

(,   )

13. Triangle IJK below is reflected in the line $y = 3$. What are the new coordinates of point J?

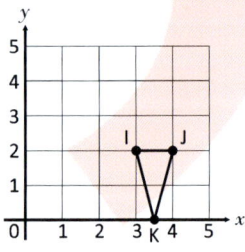

(,   )

14. Point Z at coordinates (0, 0) is translated up three units and reflected in the line $x = 5$. What are the new coordinates of point Z?

(,   )

15. Point F at coordinates (1, -3) is reflected in the x-axis. What are the new coordinates of point F?

(,   )

Chapter 14: Coordinates and Transformations - Intermediate

1. Which lettered point below is at coordinates (-4, 4)?

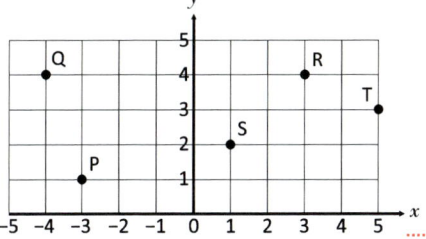

2. The two end points of a horizontal straight line have coordinates (5, y) and (11, y). What are the coordinates at the centre of the line?

(___ , ___)

3. Which of the following coordinates lie vertically to the point (-3, 9)? Circle your answer.

(3, 9)   (3, -9)   (-3, 3)   (9, -3)   (3, -3)

4. Three corner coordinates for a square are (-5, 4), (1, 4) and (1, -2). What are the coordinates of the final corner of the square?

(___ , ___)

5. What are the coordinates of the coffee shop?

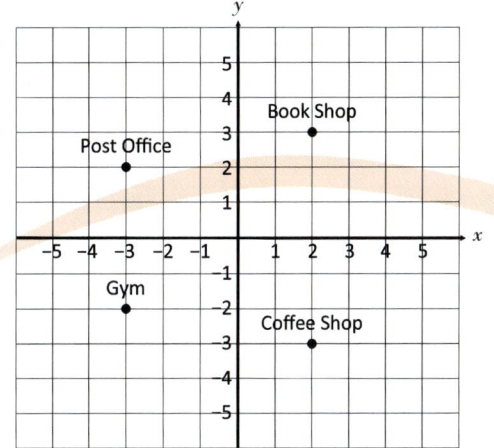

(___ , ___)

6. What are the coordinates of point C on the hexagon below?

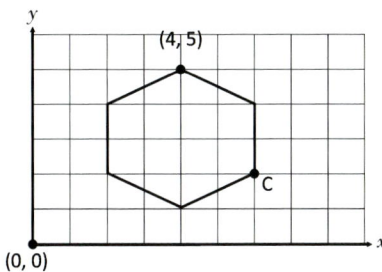

(___ , ___)

7. (-2, 3), (-2, 1) and (-4, 4) are three corners of a rhombus. What are the coordinates of the missing corner?

(___ , ___)

8. Point G at coordinates (1, 2) is rotated 180° clockwise about the point (0, 0). What are the new coordinates of point G?

(___ , ___)

9. Point T is moved 30 units left on the grid below. Which lettered point will point T now be at?

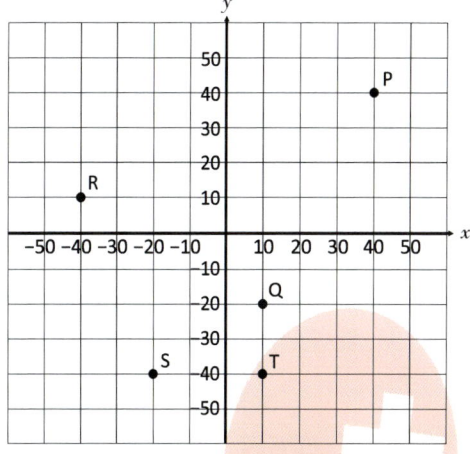

10. Point V has x-coordinate 30 and its y-coordinate is five units above -12. It is translated three units right. What are the new coordinates of point V?

(___ , ___)

11. Which letter (A to E) below shows the rectangle rotated 45° clockwise about its centre? Circle your answer.

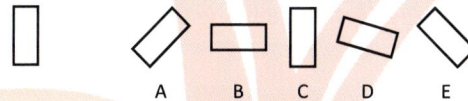

A   B   C   D   E

12. Triangle T below is reflected in line M. What are the new coordinates of point c?

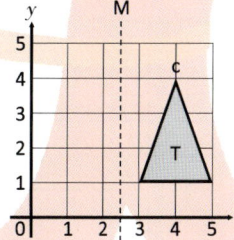

(___ , ___)

13. Which of lines L1 to L5 would point Q need to be reflected in to move it to point P?

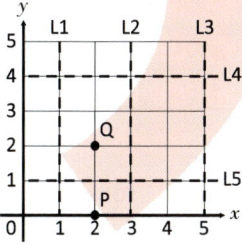

....

14. On the grid above, draw the line $y = 2$ and label it L6.

15. Shape S is rotated 90° clockwise about the point (2, 3). What are the new coordinates of point C?

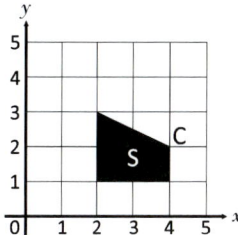

(___ , ___)

Chapter 14: Coordinates and Transformations - Advanced

1. Two corners of an isosceles triangle are (2, 1) and (15, 1). The *y*-coordinate of its final corner is -18. What are the coordinates of the final corner?

   (,   )

2. Point R is rotated 270° anticlockwise about the point (0, 0). What are the coordinates of the lettered point which is east of its new position?

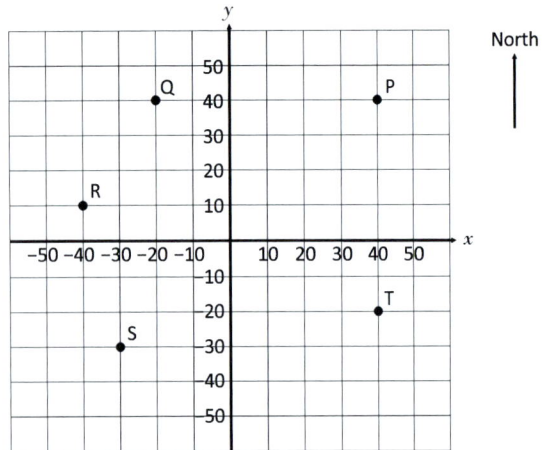

   (,   )

3. Point Z at coordinates (-5.5, -7) is translated four units left. It is then reflected in the *x*-axis. What are its new coordinates?

   (,   )

4. Shape A is reflected in the *x*-axis. Shape B is translated four units left. At which coordinates do they touch after the transformations?

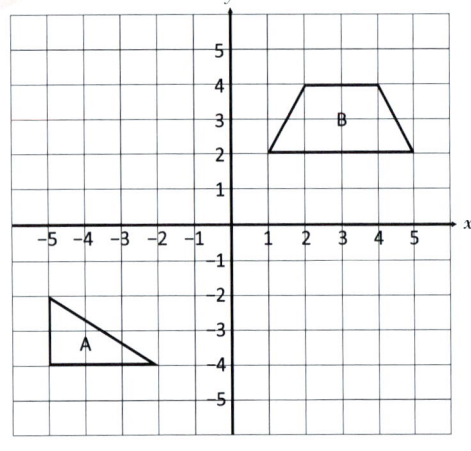

   (,   )

5. The centre coordinates for a circle are (2, 0). Its diameter is four units. What is the largest *x*-coordinate on the circumference of the circle?

   ....

6. One side of a square has corner points at coordinates (0.5, 1) and (4.5, 1). What are the two possible sets of centre coordinates of the square?

   (,   ) and (,   )

7. How many degrees clockwise does the point (1, 1) have to rotate about the origin to become (-1, 1)?

   °

8. Pentagon P is rotated 270° anticlockwise about the point (0, 3). What are the new coordinates of point C?

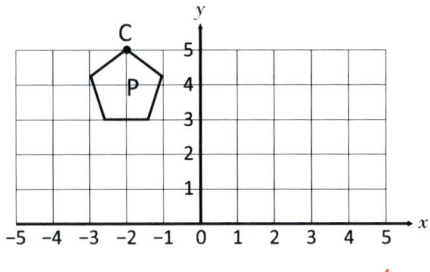

   (,   )

9. Prasha is at coordinates (4, 4). She walks in a straight line to coordinates (1, 1). She then turns through a reflex angle and walks in a straight line to coordinates (-5, 1). Both axes have the same scale. What was the size of the angle she turned through?

   °

Using the grid below, answer questions 10 to 15.

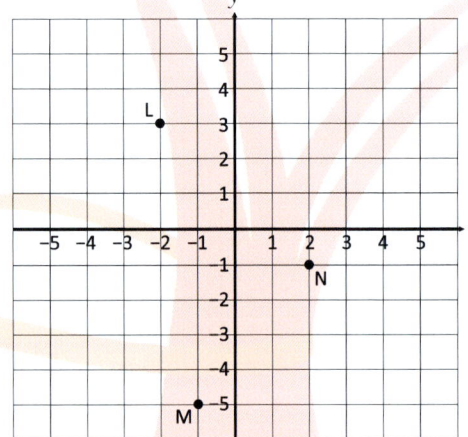

10. What are the coordinates of point N after a clockwise rotation of 180° about the point (-1, 0)?

   (,   )

11. What are the coordinates of the point halfway between point L and point N?

   (,   )

12. What is the translation that maps point M onto point N?

   ( )

13. Draw the point that is a reflection of point L in the *x*-axis and label it K.

14. Point M is translated four units right and two units up. It is then reflected in the *y*-axis. What are the new coordinates for point M?

   (,   )

15. Point N is reflected in the *x*-axis and then rotated 90° anticlockwise about the origin. What are the new coordinates for point N?

   (,   )

Answers & Explanations

Mathematics: Worded Problems

Book 1

Question	Answer	Explanation
1	**£133**	£47 + £86 = **£133**
2	340	The completed pyramid should look like this: 340 192 148 102 90 58 43 59 31 27
3	50	(23 − 7) + 34 = 16 + 34 = **50**
4	144	(9 × 8) × 2 = 72 × 2 = **144**
5	**£877.20**	Price of one laptop: £4386 ÷ 10 = £438.60 Therefore, the price of two laptops is £438.60 × 2 = **£877.20.**
6	18	Let x be the number on the card. $(x \div 6) \times 8 = 24$ $x \div 6 = 24 \div 8 = 3$ $x = 3 \times 6 = $ **18**
7	84	(4 × 12) + (4 × 9) = 48 + 36 = **84**
8	20	$(^1/_3 \times 24) + 12 = 8 + 12 = $ **20**
9	10	The completed grid should look like this: 4 5 3 6 1 **10** 3 10 2
10	12	Let x be the number Farida is thinking of. $(x \div 4) - 1 = 2$ $x \div 4 = 2 + 1 = 3$ $x = 3 \times 4 = $ **12**
11	27	Use BIDMAS: 48 − 7 × 5 + 14 = 48 − 35 + 14 = **27**
12	**120cm**	Width of rectangle: 48cm ÷ 4 = 12cm Therefore, the perimeter is (48cm × 2) + (12cm × 2) = **120cm.**
13	7	Let x be the missing number. $6x + 4 = 9x - 17$ $9x - 6x = 17 + 4$ $3x = 21$ $x = $ **7**
14	15	Number of cakes sold at school fete: $120 \times {}^3/_4 = 90$ Number of cakes sold to friends: $(120 - 90) \times {}^1/_2 = 30 \times {}^1/_2 = 15$ Therefore, there are **15** cakes left unsold.
15	29	Use BIDMAS: (84 − 63) ÷ 7 + 26 = 21 ÷ 7 + 26 = 3 + 26 = **29**

Chapter 1: Four Operations - Intermediate

Question	Answer	Explanation
1	**379**	642 − 263 = **379**
2	**3**	The sum of each row and column is 2. The completed grid should look like this: 	−5	4	**3**	 	6	2	−6	 	1	−4	5	
3	**282**	265 − 39 + 56 = **282**
4	**40**	400,000 ÷ 10,000 = **40**
5	**30**	Width of table top = 1m 20cm = 120cm Therefore, the number of blocks needed to fit across table top width is 120cm ÷ 4cm = **30.**
6	**3**	$2^3 \times \sqrt{36} \div 4^2 = 8 \times 6 \div 16 = $ **3**
7	**£16.60**	Pens: £1.75 × 7 = £12.25 Erasers: 87p × 5 = 435p = £4.35 Total: £12.25 + £4.35 = **£16.60**
8	**8,088**	Use BIDMAS: (17 − 9) × 11 + 8000 = 8 × 11 + 8000 = 88 + 8000 = **8088**
9	**4**	228 ÷ 16 = 14 R 4 Therefore, the last page must have **4** stickers.
10	**£7.40**	6 cartridges: £75.60 1 cartridge: £75.60 ÷ 6 = £12.60 £20 − £12.60 = **£7.40**
11	**38**	Total number of packets: 11 × 12 = 132 Packets sold: 42 + 52 = 94 Therefore, the number of packets remaining is 132 − 94 = **38**.
12	**10**	Equation 1: 6 × 9 − C = 47 → 54 − C = 47 → 54 − 47 = C = 7 Now, substitute C = 7 into equation 2. Equation 2: 24 ÷ 8 + 7 = R = **10**
13	**13**	Use BIDMAS: (130 − 39) ÷ (4 + 3) = 91 ÷ 7 = **13**
14	**£105.00**	£85 + (24 × £27.50) = £745 £745 − £640 = **£105**
15	**5**	P = 14 − 5 × 2 + 8 = 14 − 10 + 8 = 12 Q = −2 + 18 ÷ 6 + 16 = −2 + 3 + 16 = 17 Q − P = 17 − 12 = **5**

Chapter 1: Four Operations - Advanced

Question	Answer	Explanation
1	**594,733**	287,988 + 306,745 = **594,733**
2	**1,869**	4837 – 2968 = **1869**
3	**1,224km**	London to New Delhi: 6718km London to New Delhi (via Cairo): 3513km + 4429km = 7942km 7942km – 6718km = **1224km**
4	**312kg**	Mass of pickles in one box: 520g × 12 = 6240g Therefore, the mass of pickles in one full crate is 6240g × 50 = 312000g = **312kg**.
5	**£24.50**	£1029 ÷ 42 = **£24.50**
6	**24cm**	2.16m ÷ 9 = 0.24m = **24cm**
7	**£527.49**	£234.99 + (£48.75 × 6) = £234.99 + £292.50 = **£527.49**
8	**7,900kg**	Weight of elephant: 140,000 × 45g = 6,300,000g = 6300kg Therefore, the combined weight is 1600kg + 6300kg = **7900kg**.
9	**367.5l**	420,000ml × $\frac{7}{8}$ = 367,500ml = **367.5l**
10	**£6.40**	Original price of individual toy: £153 ÷ 34 = £4.50 Therefore, the new price for each toy is £4.50 + £1.90 = **£6.40**.
11	**78**	USE BIDMAS: (3 + 9) × 7 – 18 ÷ 3 = 12 × 7 – 6 = 84 – 6 = **78**
12	**53.76m^2**	(12.8m × 2) + (width × 2) = 25.6m + (width × 2) = 34m Width = (34m – 25.6m) ÷ 2 = 4.2m Area of pool: length × width = 12.8m × 4.2m = **53.76m^2**
13	**36**	Let x be the missing number. 38 – 3 × 5 = x ÷ 4 + 14 38 – 15 = 23 = x ÷ 4 + 14 x = (23 – 14) × 4 = **36**
14	**10**	For the purposes of 11 plus, we have excluded 0 as a cube or square number. Second cube number: 8. Third triangular number: 6. ((7 × 8) + 4) ÷ 6 = (56 + 4) ÷ 6 = 60 ÷ 6 = **10**
15	**1.375**	Number of slices sold: £41.48 ÷ 68p = 61 Number of unsold slices: (9 × 8) – 61 = 72 – 61 = 11 Therefore, the number of unsold cakes is 11 ÷ 8 = **1.375**.

Question	Answer	Explanation
1	**7,298**	7 thousand + 2 hundred + 9 tens + 8 units 7000 + 200 + 90 + 8 = **7298**
2	**ten thousand and three**	10 thousand + 3 units ten thousand and three
3	**1) 55,605 2) 55,616 3) 55,661 4) 56,165 5) 56,516**	Ascending order means going up in order of increasing value.
4	**4,206**	4 thousand + 2 hundred + 6 units 4000 + 200 + 6 = **4206**
5	**£4,000**	In the price, £14,738, the 4 is in the thousands column and is therefore worth **£4000**.
6	**20,000**	The 2 is in the ten thousands column and is therefore equal to **20,000.**
7	**69kg**	The number 7 (tenths column) is ≥ 5, so the number 8 (units column) is rounded up to 9 to give **69kg** to the nearest kilogram.
8	**94.6**	The number 3 (hundredths column) is < 5, so the number 6 (tenths column) remains the same to give **94.6** to the nearest tenth.
9	**72**	$9(8) = 9 \times 8 = $ **72**
10	**15**	n^{th} rule: $3n$ Therefore, the 5th term is $3(5) = 3 \times 5 = $ **15**.
11	**6n**	The common difference is +6, so the nth rule takes the form $6n + x$. $6(1) + x = 6$ so $x = 0$. Therefore, the nth rule is **6n**.
12	**−7**	The common difference is +7. Therefore, the missing term is $−14 + 7 = $ **−7**.
13	**10 − 5n**	The common difference is −5, so the nth rule takes the form $−5n + x$. $−5(1) + x = 5$ so $x = 10$. Therefore, the nth rule is $−5n + 10$, which can be written as **10 − 5n**.
14	**29**	The common difference is +3, so the nth rule takes the form $3n + x$. $3(1) + x = 1$ so $x = −2$. n^{th} rule: $3n − 2$ 5th term: $3(5) − 2 = 13$ 6th term: $3(6) − 2 = 16$ Therefore, the number of squares needed is $13 + 16 = $ **29**.
15	**1.11**	The common difference is +0.02. Therefore, the next term is $1.09 + 0.02 = $ **1.11**.

Question	Answer	Explanation
1	**426,938**	426 thousand + 9 hundred + 3 tens + 8 units 426,000 + 900 + 30 + 8 = **426,938**
2	**seven hundred and thirty thousand, eight hundred and five**	700 thousand + 30 thousand + 0 thousand + 8 hundred + 0 tens + 5 units **seven hundred and thirty thousand, eight hundred and five**
3	**338,039**	In ascending order: 1) 309,839 2) 330,893 3) 338,039 4) 338,308 5) 338,903. Therefore, the third largest is **338,039** (third number from the right).
4	**428,012**	400,000 + 28,012 = **428,012**
5	**80,000**	In the number 5$\underline{8}$5,495, the underlined 8 is in the ten thousands column and is therefore worth **80,000**.
6	**321.42**	The number 6 (third decimal place) is ≥ 5, so the number 1 (second decimal place) is rounded up to 2 to give **321.42** to two decimal places.
7	**£3,000**	£29.45 × 100 = £2945 The number 9 (hundreds column) is ≥ 5, so the number 2 (thousands column) is rounded up to 3 to give **£3000** to the nearest £1000.
8	**42**	The number of squares in a pattern is 4 more than the previous pattern. As the 4th pattern has 13 squares, the 5th, 6th and 7th patterns must have 17, 21 and 25 squares respectively. Sum of 5th and 7th = 17 + 25 = **42** squares.
9	**0.01**	7007 ÷ N = 700,700 Therefore, N = 7007 ÷ 700,700 = **0.01**.
10	**$2n + 1$**	The common difference is +2, so the nth rule takes the form $2n + x$. $2(1) + x = 3$ so $x = 1$. Therefore, the nth rule is **$2n + 1$**.
11	**5**	5th term: 5(5) − 4 = 21 6th term: 5(6) − 4 = 26 Therefore, the difference between the terms is 26 − 21 = **5**.
12	**$1\,^7/_8$**	The common difference is $+^4/_8$. Therefore, the missing term is $1\,^3/_8 + {}^4/_8 = \mathbf{1\,^7/_8}$.
13	**shaded**	Number of circles in pattern: 7 Number of full patterns: 29 ÷ 7 = 4 R 1 → 1 remaining circle The 29th circle is the first circle of pattern 5 and is therefore **shaded.**
14	**13**	The common difference is −4, so the nth rule takes the form $-4n + x$. $-4(5) + x = -3$ so $x = 17$. n^{th} rule: $-4n + 17$ Therefore, the 1st term is $-4(1) + 17 = \mathbf{13}$.
15	**25**	There are two sequences: odd numbered terms are a sequence of square numbers and even numbered terms are a sequence of prime numbers. The next term (9th) is odd therefore it is the square number after 16 → **25**.

Question	Answer	Explanation
1	ninety-two million, nine hundred and fifty-five thousand, eight hundred and seven	90 million + 2 million + 900 thousand + 50 thousand + 5 thousand + 8 hundred + 0 tens + 7 units **ninety-two million, nine hundred and fifty-five thousand, eight hundred and seven**
2	6,626,246	In descending order: 1) 3,331,131 2) 3,313,133 3) 3,313,113 4) 3,313,031 5) 3,113,113. Therefore, the sum of the second and third largest is 3,313,133 + 3,313,113 = **6,626,246**.
3	83,704,603	83,000,000 + 704,000 + 600 + 3 = **83,704,603**
4	40,000,000	645,037,189 = 6$\underline{4}$5 million + 37 thousand + 1 hundred + 8 tens + 9 units 6$\underline{4}$5 million = 600 million + $\underline{40\ \text{million}}$ + 5 million The underlined 4 is in the 10 million column and is therefore worth **40,000,000**.
5	200,950,000	718,238,650 − 518,238,650 = 200,000,000 1,950,000 − 1,000,000 = 950,000 Therefore, the sum of the two answers is 200,000,000 + 950,000 = **200,950,000**.
6	22	The number 7 (tens column) is ≥ 5, so the 8 (hundreds column) is rounded up to 9 to give 126,900 to the nearest 100. Therefore, the difference is 126,900 − 126,878 = **22**.
7	3.142	The number 5 (fourth decimal place) is ≥ 5, so the number 1 (third decimal place) is rounded up to 2 to give **3.142** to three decimal places.
8	109	Sun's diameter rounded to the nearest 100 = 864,900 Earth's diameter rounded to the nearest 100 = 7900 Number of Earths that can fit across the Sun : 864,900 ÷ 7900 = 109.481… → **109**.
9	110	The common difference is +4, so the nth rule takes the form $4n + x$. $4(1) + x = 6$ so $x = 2$. n^{th} rule: $4n + 2$ Therefore, the 27th term is $4(27) + 2 = 108 + 2 = $ **110**.
10	35	n^{th} rule: $4n + 2$ $4n + 2 = 142$ $n = (142 − 2) ÷ 4 = $ **35**
11	−25	The common difference is +7. Therefore, the 1st term is −18 − 7 = **−25**.
12	3 $^3/_5$	$3(6)/_5 = 18/_5 = $ **3 $3/_5$**
13	$3n + 1$	The common difference is +3, so the nth rule takes the form $3n + x$. $3(1) + x = 4$ so $x = 1$. Therefore, the nth rule is **$3n + 1$**.
14	B	Number of triangles in pattern: 6 Number of full patterns: 86 ÷ 6 = 14 R 2 → 2 remaining triangles The second triangle in the pattern contains the letter **B**.
15	21	There are two sequences: odd numbered terms are a sequence of triangular numbers and even numbered terms are a sequence of doubling numbers. The next term (11th) is odd, therefore it is the triangular number after 15 → **21**.

Chapter 3: Factors and Multiples - Beginner

Question	Answer	Explanation
1	**25**	**25** divides into 300 exactly 12 times.
2	**1, 2, 3, 6**	Any whole number that divides exactly into a whole number N is termed a factor. This includes 1 and the number N itself. The factors of 6 are **1**, **2**, **3** and **6**.
3	**4**	The numbers in the grid that are factors of 24 are 8, 24, 1 and 3.
4	**1 and 5**	Factors of 10: **1**, 2, **5**, 10 Factors of 15: **1**, 3, **5**, 15 The common factors are shown above in **bold**.
5	**17**	Factors of 12: 1, 2, 3, 4, 6, 12 2 + 3 + 12 = **17**
6	**3**	Factors of 6: 1, 2, **3**, 6 Factors of 9: 1, **3**, 9 The HCF (shown in **bold**) is **3**.
7	**54**	9 × 6 = 54 **54** is the only multiple of 9 between 47 and 61.
8	**58**	The last house number will be the 29th even number. 29 × 2 = **58**
9	**42**	First three multiples of 7: 7, 14, 21 7 + 14 + 21 = **42**
10	**8**	The grid contains multiples of 8. The missing multiple is 8 × 1 = **8**.
11	**240**	Number of bottles in a box: 6 × 10 = 60 Therefore, the number of bottles in 4 boxes is 60 × 4 = **240**.
12	**15**	Multiples of 3: 3, 6, 9, 12, **15**, 18, 21... Multiples of 5: 5, 10, **15**, 20, 25, 30, 35... The LCM (shown in **bold**) is **15**.
13	**8**	16 ÷ 8 = 2 4 × 2 = 8 Therefore, **8** is both a factor of 16 and a multiple of 4.
14	**3, 6, 9, 18**	Factors of 18: 1, 2, **3, 6, 9, 18** The multiples of 3 are shown above in **bold**.
15	**15**	Factors of 45: 1, 3, 5, 9, 15, 45 The factors that are between 8 and 40 are 9 and 15. Of the two, **15** is the only multiple of 5.

Chapter 3: Factors and Multiples - Intermediate

Question	Answer	Explanation
1	1, 2, 3, 6, 9, 18, 27, 54	Any whole number that divides exactly into a whole number N is termed a factor. This includes 1 and the number N itself. The factors of 54 are **1, 2, 3, 6, 9, 18, 27** and **54**.
2	432, 289, 980, 1,885	A composite number is a whole number that can be divided evenly by numbers other than 1 or itself. From the list, the composite numbers are **432, 289, 980** and **1885**.
3	T	Factors of 36: **1, 2, 3, 4, 6**, 9, **12**, 18, 36 Factors of 48: **1, 2, 3, 4, 6**, 8, **12**, 16, 24, 48 The common factors shown above in **bold** form a **T** shape in the grid.
4	19	Factors of 34: 1, **2, 17**, 34. The prime factors are shown above in **bold**. Therefore, the sum of the prime factors is 2 + 17 = **19**.
5	14	Factors of 42: 1, 2, 3, 6, 7, **14**, 21, 42 Factors of 56: 1, 2, 4, 7, 8, **14**, 28, 56 The HCF (shown in **bold**) is **14**.
6	2, 5, 7	Factors of 70: 1, **2, 5, 7**, 10, 14, 35, 70 The prime factors are shown above in **bold**.
7	170	As the 4th multiple of 34 is 4 × 34 = 136, the 5th multiple of 34 must be between 138 and 200. 5 × 34 = **170**
8	90, 138, 168	Chair numbers in the list that are divisible by 6 with no remainder make complete sets, these are **90, 138** and **168**.
9	60	Number of apples (bags of 12) in one full box: 12 × 20 = 240 If only 4 apples are packed in each bag, each full box will contain 240 ÷ 4 = **60** bags.
10	85	The numbers in the rows and columns in the table are based on multiples of 17 starting with 1 × 17 = 17 in the top left square. The 5th multiple of 17 i.e. 5 × 17 = **85** is the multiple missing in the bottom right corner square.
11	180	Number of tables for 4: $^{3}/_{4}$ × 40 = 3 × 10 = 30, 30 × 4 = 120 diners Number of tables for 6: 40 − 30 = 10, 10 × 6 = 60 diners Therefore, the total number of diners is 120 + 60 = **180**.
12	60	Multiples of 12: 12, 24, 36, 48, **60**, 72… Multiples of 15: 15, 30, 45, **60**, 75, 90… The LCM (shown in **bold**) is **60**.
13	27	Factors of 81: 1, 3, 9, **27**, 81 Multiples of 9: 9, 18, **27**, 36, 45, 54, 63, 72, 81… From the numbers in the list only **27** is a factor of 81 and a multiple of 9.
14	100 and 1100	Factors of 44: <u>1</u>, 2, 4, <u>11</u>, 22, 44 Factors of 55: <u>1</u>, 5, <u>11</u>, 55 100th multiple of 1 is 1 × 100 = **100** and 100th multiple of 11 is 11 × 100 = **1100**.
15	12	3 digit multiples of 7 less than 130: …105, 112, 119, <u>126</u>… 3 digit multiples of 9 less than 130: …108, 117, <u>126</u>… Factors of 126 are 1, 2, 3, 6, 7, 9, 14, 18, 21, 42, 63 and 126 → **12 factors**.

Chapter 3: Factors and Multiples - Advanced

Question	Answer	Explanation
1	**1, 2, 3 and 6**	Factors of 36: **1**, **2**, **3**, 4, **6**, 9, 12, 18, 36 Factors of 54: **1**, **2**, **3**, **6**, 9, 18, 27, 54 Factors of 96: **1**, **2**, **3**, 4, **6**, 8, 12, 16, 24, 32, 48, 96 The common factors are shown above in **bold**.
2	**2, 7, 17**	Factors of 238: 1, **2**, **7**, 14, **17**, 34, 119, 238 The prime factors are shown above in **bold**.
3	**1, 2, 13, 26**	Numbers in the shaded area are factors common to both 52 and 78. Factors of 52: **1**, **2**, 4, **13**, **26**, 52 Factors of 78: **1**, **2**, 3, 6, **13**, **26**, 39, 78 The common factors are shown above in **bold**.
4	**9**	To form a trebling sequence and also sum to 13, the factor numbers must be small in value. 2, 6, 18 gives a trebling sequence but a total > 13. 1, 3 and 9 are the correct factors as they sum to 13 and have a trebling sequence. The number must therefore be **9** which has factors of 1, 3 and 9.
5	**39**	Factors of 40: 1, 2, 4, 5, 8, 10, **20**, 40 Factors of 100: 1, 2, 4, 5, 10, **20**, 25, 50, 100 The HCF (shown in **bold**) is **20**. Factors of 57: 1, 3, **19**, 57 Factors of 76: 1, 2, 4, **19**, 38, 76 The HCF (shown in **bold**) is **19**. Therefore, the sum of the HCFs is 20 + 19 = **39**.
6	**44**	As the six factors of N must include 1, five factors of N are actually known. They are 1, 2, 4, 11 and 22. Multiplying factor pairs gives 1 × N, 2 × 22 and 4 × 11. Two of the three pairs multiply out to 44. Therefore, N must be **44** to give 1 × 44 = 44.
7	**664**	Trying the 10th multiple of 83 gives 10 × 83 = 830 (too large). Try the 8th multiple of 83 which gives 8 × 83 = **664,** which is between 590 and 730.
8	**232**	Head table: 12 guests Number of tables seating 4: $(^4/_5)$ × 50 = 40 → 40 × 4 = 160 guests Number of tables seating 6: 50 − 40 = 10 → 10 × 6 = 60 guests Therefore, the total number of guests is 12 + 160 + 60 = **232**.
9	**40**	Multiples of 4: 4, 8, 12, 16, 20, 24, 28, 32, 36, **40**, 44... Multiples of 5: 5, 10, 15, 20, 25, 30, 35, **40**, 45... Multiples of 8: 8, 16, 24, 32, **40**, 48... The LCM (shown in **bold**) is **40**.
10	**96**	8th multiple of 84: 8 × 84 = 672 As 672 = 7 × the number required, the number required = 672 ÷ 7 = **96**.
11	**532**	The numbers in the rows and columns in the table are based on multiples of 76. As 304, shown in the table, is the 4th multiple of 76, moving to the right gives the 5th multiple of 76 i.e. 5 × 76 = 380 in 3 squares, the 6th multiple of 76 i.e. 6 × 76 = 456 in 2 squares, and finally, the 7th multiple of 76 i.e. 7 × 76 = **532** in the bottom right corner square.

Question	Answer	Explanation
12	210	Multiples of 30: 30, 60, 90, 120, 150, 180, **210**, 240... Multiples of 42: 42, 84, 126, 168, **210**, 252... The LCM (shown in **bold**) is **210**.
13	392	As the 8 factors must include 1, 7 factors are actually known. They are 1, 2, 4, 7, 8, 14 and 28. Multiplying factor pairs gives 1 × ?, 2 × 28, 4 × 14 and 7 × 8. Three of the four pairs multiply out to 56. Therefore ? must be 56 to give 1 × 56 = 56. The number required is the 7th multiple of 56 which is 7 × 56 = **392**, and the sum of the digits is 14 as required.
14	36	First 10 multiples of 12: 12, 24, **36**, 48, 60, **72**, 84, 96, **108**, 120 First 10 multiples of 18: 18, **36**, 54, **72**, 90, **108**, 126, 144, 162, 180 Multiples common to 12 and 18 (shown in **bold**) are **36**, **72** and **108**. Factors of 36: 1, 2, 3, 4, 6, 9, 12, 18, **36** Factors of 72: 1, 2, 3, 4, 6, 8, 9, 12, 18, 24, **36**, 72 Factors of 108: 1, 2, 3, 4, 6, 9, 12, 18, 27, **36**, 54, 108 The HCF (shown in **bold**) is **36**.
15	(a) 4 (b) 60 (c) 2, 3, 5 (d) 30	Factors of 28: 1, 2, **4**, 7, 14, 28 Factors of 52: 1, 2, **4**, 13, 26, 52 Factors of 68: 1, 2, **4**, 17, 34, 68 The HCF (shown in **bold**) is **4** (answer a). The 15th multiple of answer a is 15 × 4 = **60** (answer b). The 3 different prime factors of 60 are **2**, **3** and **5** (answer c). Multiples of 2: 2, 4, 6, 8, 10, 12, 14, 16, 18, 20, 22, 24, 26, 28, **30**, 32... Multiples of 3: 3, 6, 9, 12, 15, 18, 21, 24, 27, **30**, 33... Multiples of 5: 5, 10, 15, 20, 25, **30**, 35... The LCM (shown in **bold**) is **30** (answer d).

Question	Answer	Explanation
1	$\frac{1}{3}$ and $\frac{2}{6}$	$\frac{2}{6}$ simplifies down to $\frac{1}{3}$ in lowest terms, making them equivalent fractions.
2	$\frac{3}{4}$	6 out of 8 sectors are shaded in grey, which as a fraction is $\frac{6}{8} = \frac{3}{4}$.
3	3	$8 \div 2 = 4$ Therefore, the missing number is $12 \div 4 = \mathbf{3}$.
4	$\frac{2}{5}$ and $\frac{10}{25}$	Shape on LHS: 2 parts shaded out of 5 = $\frac{2}{5}$ Shape on RHS: 10 parts shaded out of 25 = $\frac{10}{25}$ $\frac{2}{5}$ and $\frac{10}{25}$ are equivalent fractions.
5	$\frac{5}{6}$	$\frac{1}{2} + \frac{1}{3} = \frac{3}{6} + \frac{2}{6} = \mathbf{\frac{5}{6}}$
6	$\frac{2}{5}$	$\frac{3}{5} \times \frac{2}{3} = \frac{6}{15} = \mathbf{\frac{2}{5}}$
7	£33.00	The number 7 (tenths column) is ≥ 5, so the number 2 (units column) is rounded up to 3 to give **£33** to the nearest £1.
8	6.39	$63.9 \div 10 = \mathbf{6.39}$
9	0.24l	The number 4 (third decimal place) is < 5, so the number 4 (second decimal place) remains the same to give **0.24l** to two decimal places.
10	258	$2.58 \times 100 = \mathbf{258}$
11	4.86kg	$0.54\text{kg} \times 9 = \mathbf{4.86kg}$
12	4.57l	$36.56\text{l} \div 8 = \mathbf{4.57l}$
13	0.75	The largest fraction is $\frac{3}{4}$. $3 \div 4 = \mathbf{0.75}$
14	1.1	$\frac{7}{10} + \frac{2}{5} = \frac{7}{10} + \frac{4}{10} = \frac{11}{10} = 11 \div 10 = \mathbf{1.1}$
15	2.375	$2\frac{1}{2} - \frac{1}{8} = 2.5 - 0.125 = \mathbf{2.375}$

Chapter 4: Fractions and Decimals - Intermediate

Question	Answer	Explanation
1	$^{16}/_{20}$, $^{12}/_{15}$, $^{64}/_{80}$	$^{16}/_{20}$, $^{12}/_{15}$ and $^{64}/_{80}$ each simplify down to $^{4}/_{5}$ in their lowest terms and are therefore equivalent fractions.
2	$^{7}/_{12}$, $^{3}/_{5}$, $^{5}/_{8}$, $^{3}/_{4}$, $^{7}/_{8}$	From left to right the fractions are $^{14}/_{24}$, $^{3}/_{5}$, $^{14}/_{16}$, $^{6}/_{8}$ and $^{5}/_{8}$. These reduce down to $^{7}/_{12}$, $^{3}/_{5}$, $^{7}/_{8}$, $^{3}/_{4}$ and $^{5}/_{8}$. In ascending size order they are $^{7}/_{12}$, $^{3}/_{5}$, $^{5}/_{8}$, $^{3}/_{4}$ and $^{7}/_{8}$.
3	$^{5}/_{16}$	Sum the two fractions and divide the result by 2 to find the halfway value. $^{3}/_{8} + ^{1}/_{4} = ^{3}/_{8} + ^{2}/_{8} = ^{5}/_{8}$ $^{5}/_{8} \div 2 = ^{5}/_{8} \times ^{1}/_{2} = ^{5}/_{16}$
4	$^{17}/_{20}$ and $^{85}/_{100}$	Observe from diagrams that equivalent fractions are $^{17}/_{20}$ and $^{85}/_{100}$. Note $^{85}/_{100}$ is $^{17}/_{20}$ in its lowest terms.
5	$2\,^{3}/_{4}$	$8\,^{3}/_{8} - 5\,^{5}/_{8} = ^{67}/_{8} - ^{45}/_{8} = ^{22}/_{8} = \mathbf{2\,^{3}/_{4}}$ in lowest terms
6	$^{3}/_{35}$	$6/_{7} \div 10 = 6/_{7} \times 1/_{10} = 6/_{70} = \mathbf{3/_{35}}$
7	37,100g	1kg = 1000g so 37.096kg = 37096g. The number 9 (tens column) is ≥ 5, so the number 0 (hundreds column) is increased by 1 giving **37100g** to the nearest 100g.
8	£6.10	Amount Prasha paid: 4 × £20 = £80 Change received: £80 − £73.92 = £6.08 Therefore, to the nearest 10p this is **£6.10**.
9	907.2	Cancel out the same number of 0s i.e. four, top and bottom to leave 9.072 × 100 which gives **907.2**.
10	210cm	10mm = 1cm so 2096mm = 209.6cm. The number 6 (tenths column) is ≥ 5, so the number 9 (units column) is increased by 1 giving **210cm** to the nearest cm.
11	152.4cm	As 1ft = 0.3048m, 5ft in metres is 5 × 0.3048m = 1.524m. 1m = 100cm so 1.524m = **152.4cm**.
12	50.7cm	Shaded area length: 29.7cm ÷ 2 = 14.85cm Shaded area width: 21cm ÷ 2 = 10.5cm Therefore, the perimeter is (2 × 14.85cm) + (2 × 10.5cm) = **50.7cm**.
13	8.685	Divide 685 by 1000 to express in decimal form, giving 0.685. Therefore, the total number in decimal form is 8 + 0.685 = **8.685**.
14	(a) 0.3125 (b) 20	**(a)** Number of pages with at least 1 picture: $^{3}/_{8} + ^{5}/_{16} = ^{6}/_{16} + ^{5}/_{16} = ^{11}/_{16}$ Therefore, the fraction of pages without a picture is $1 - ^{11}/_{16} = ^{5}/_{16}$. As a decimal, $^{5}/_{16} = 5 \div 16 = \mathbf{0.3125}$. **(b)** Pages without a picture: $^{5}/_{16} \times 64 = \mathbf{20}$
15	$^{321}/_{50}$	$6.42 = 6 + ^{42}/_{100} = 6 + ^{21}/_{50} = \mathbf{^{321}/_{50}}$

Chapter 4: Fractions and Decimals - Advanced

Question	Answer	Explanation
1	<	LHS: $^5/_9 + {^2/_3} = {^5/_9} + {^6/_9} = {^{11}/_9} \approx 1.22$ RHS: $^4/_5 + {^7/_{10}} = {^8/_{10}} + {^7/_{10}} = {^{15}/_{10}} = {^3/_2} = 1.5$ 1.22 < 1.5
2	$^{22}/_{25}$	Convert to cm: 180mm = 18cm, 1.5m = 150cm Length of wood left on strip: 150cm − 18cm = 132cm Fraction of the original strip length = $^{132}/_{150} = {^{66}/_{75}} = \mathbf{^{22}/_{25}}$
3	$4\ ^{17}/_{40}$	$8\ ^{225}/_{1000} - 3\ {^4/_5} = 8\ {^{225}/_{1000}} - 3\ {^{800}/_{1000}} = {^{8225}/_{1000}} - {^{3800}/_{1000}} = {^{4425}/_{1000}}$ $^{4425}/_{1000} = 4\ {^{425}/_{1000}} = \mathbf{4\ ^{17}/_{40}}$
4	34	Number of cards held by Mel : $^2/_3 \times 12 = 8$ Number of cards held by Alex : $1\ ^1/_6 \times 12 = {^7/_6} \times 12 = 14$ Therefore, the number of cards held by all three players is 12 + 8 + 14 = **34**.
5	£1,100	$^3/_5 \times ? = £660$ $3 \times ? = £660 \times 5 = £3300$ Therefore, the answer is £3300 ÷ 3 = **£1100**.
6	$3\ ^1/_3$	$(2\ ^2/_9 \times 6) \div 4 = ({^{20}/_9} \times 6) \div 4 = {^{40}/_3} \div 4 = {^{40}/_3} \times {^1/_4} = {^{40}/_{12}} = {^{10}/_3} = \mathbf{3\ ^1/_3}$
7	0.4	7.184 − ? = 6.784 Therefore, the answer is 7.184 − 6.784 = **0.4**.
8	84.726	The number 4 (fourth decimal place) is < 5, so the number 6 (third decimal place) remains the same. Therefore, 84.726439 rounded to three decimal places is **84.726**.
9	(a) 2.398m^2 (b) 23,980cm^2	Area of rectangle = length × width **(a)** 2.18m × 1.1m = **2.398m^2** **(b)** To convert m^2 to cm^2, multiply by 10,000. Therefore, the area is 2.398m^2 × 10000 = **23980cm^2**.
10	0.15 miles	The car travels 54 miles in 1 hour or 3,600 seconds. Miles travelled per second: $^{54}/_{3600} = {^3/_{200}} = 0.015$ miles Therefore, the number of miles travelled in 10 seconds is 0.015 × 10 = **0.15 miles**.
11	(a) $2\ ^2/_3$ (b) $^8/_3$ (c) 2.67	(a) $1 + 1 + {^4/_6} = 2\ {^4/_6} = \mathbf{2\ ^2/_3}$ (b) $2\ ^2/_3 = \mathbf{^8/_3}$ (c) 8 ÷ 3 = 2.6666... = **2.67** (to 2 decimal places)
12	0.62	$^1/_5 \times 3\ {^1/_{10}} = {^1/_5} \times {^{31}/_{10}} = {^{31}/_{50}} = 31 \div 50 = \mathbf{0.62}$
13	$14\ ^{57}/_{80}$	$14.7125 = 14\ {^{7125}/_{10000}} = 14\ {^{285}/_{400}} = \mathbf{14\ ^{57}/_{80}}$
14	5.8	$3\ ^5/_{12} + 2\ {^3/_8} = 3\ {^{10}/_{24}} + 2\ {^9/_{24}} = 5\ {^{19}/_{24}}$ 19 ÷ 24 = 0.7916666... = 0.8 (to nearest tenth) Therefore, $5\ ^{19}/_{24}$ expressed as a decimal is 5 + 0.8 = **5.8**.
15	37.5%	£20 − £12.50 = £7.50 (£7.50 ÷ £20) × 100 = 0.375 × 100 = **37.5%**

Question	Answer	Explanation
1	7	70 × 10% = 70 × 0.1 = **7**
2	20	100% − 80% = 20% = 0.2 100 × 0.2 = **20**
3	£380.00	£400 × 5% = £400 × 0.05 = £20 Therefore, the reduced price is £400 − £20 = **£380**.
4	1kg	5kg × 20% = 5kg × 0.2 = **1kg**
5	60%	$^6/_{10}$ = $^{60}/_{100}$ = **60%**
6	3:4	Divide each ratio part by 2 to get **3:4**.
7	7:5	The ratio of red beads to blue beads is 21:15. Divide each ratio part by 3 to get **7:5**.
8	3:1	The ratio of shaded slices to unshaded slices is 6:2. Divide each ratio part by 2 to get **3:1**.
9	9	The ratio of yellow counters to green counters is 4:3. 4:3 is equivalent to 12:G (where G represents the number of green counters). 12 ÷ 4 = 3 so G = 3 × 3 = **9**.
10	12	The ratio of crosses to dots is 3:2. 3:2 is equivalent to 18:D (where D represents the number of dots). 18 ÷ 3 = 6 so D = 2 × 6 = **12**.
11	25%	$^{20}/_{80}$ = $^2/_8$ = $^1/_4$ = **25%**
12	350g	Butter required for one person: 500g ÷ 10 = 50g Therefore, a cake for seven people will require 50g × 7 = **350g**.
13	80	$^4/_5$ × 100 = 0.8 × 100 = **80**
14	28km	7cm ÷ 1cm = 7 Therefore, the real distance is 4km × 7 = **28km**.
15	8m	If the scale is 1:200, the real length of the room is 4cm × 200 = 800cm = **8m**.

Question	Answer	Explanation
1	**420g**	600g × 70% = 600g × 0.7 = **420g**
2	**£16.50**	£15 × 10% = £15 × 0.1 = £1.50 Therefore, the new price is £15 + £1.50 = **£16.50**.
3	**60%**	$^3/_5$ × 100 = 3 × 20 = **60%**
4	**20%**	Fraction of shaded bricks: $^5/_{25}$ $^5/_{25}$ × 100 = 5 × 4 = **20%**
5	**30**	Tickets sold to men: 150 × 50% = 150 × 0.5 = 75 Tickets sold to women: 150 × 30% = 150 × 0.3 = 45 Therefore, the remaining number of tickets is 150 − (75 + 45) = 150 − 120 = **30**.
6	**27**	30 × 90% = 30 × $^{90}/_{100}$ = 9 × 3 = **27**
7	**6:5**	The ratio of tea to coffee drinkers is 12:10. Divide each ratio part by 2 to get **6:5**.
8	**7:12**	Divide each ratio part by 6 to get **7:12**.
9	**12**	Dividing the total number of grapes by the sum of ratio parts gives 28 ÷ (4 + 3) = 4. Therefore, the number of grapes given to John is 4 × 3 = **12**.
10	**2:3**	The ratio of shaded to unshaded circles is 6:9. Divide each ratio part by 3 to get **2:3**.
11	$^3/_5$	The proportion of shaded squares is $^6/_{10}$ = $^3/_5$.
12	**35**	The ratio of silver to blue cars sold is 9:5. 9:5 is equivalent to 63:B (where B represents the number of blue cars sold). 63 ÷ 9 = 7 so B = 5 × 7 = **35**.
13	**3.5 miles**	Number of miles train travels in 1 minute: 8 ÷ 16 = 0.5 miles Therefore, the number of miles the train travels in 7 minutes is 7 × 0.5 miles = **3.5 miles**.
14	**36**	Cost of one packet: £7.50 ÷ 6 = £1.25 Therefore, the number of packets in a box is £45 ÷ £1.25 = **36**.
15	**7cm**	As the scale is 1:2000, the length of the line is 140m ÷ 2000 = 0.07m = **7cm**.

Question	Answer	Explanation
1	**67%**	$^{201}/_{300} \times 100 = {}^{201}/_3 =$ **67%**
2	**£10.80**	£15 × 72% = £15 × 0.72 = **£10.80**
3	**9**	3% = 3 ÷ 100 = 0.03 N × 0.03 = 0.27 Therefore, N is 0.27 ÷ 0.03 = 27 ÷ 3 = **9**.
4	**31.25%**	There are 16 pieces in total. Number of pieces eaten: $16 \times (^1/_8 + {}^1/_8 + {}^7/_{16}) = 16 \times (^2/_{16} + {}^2/_{16} + {}^7/_{16})$ $= 16 \times {}^{11}/_{16} = 11$ Number of uneaten pieces: 16 − 11 = 5 Therefore, the percentage of uneaten pieces is $^5/_{16} \times 100 = {}^{500}/_{16} = {}^{125}/_4 =$ **31.25%**.
5	**£11.28**	Amount of interest added: £720 × 2.6% = £720 × 0.026 = £18.72 Therefore, the amount remaining is £750 − (£720 + £18.72) = £750 − £738.72 = **£11.28**.
6	**1:3:7**	Divide each ratio part by 2 to get **1:3:7**.
7	**13:9:8**	1.5m = 150cm Length of L3: 150cm − (65cm + 45cm) = 150cm − 110cm = 40cm Therefore, the ratio L1 to L2 to L3 is 65:45:40 = **13:9:8**.
8	**4:5**	960g:1.2kg = 960g:1200g = 96g:120g Divide each ratio part by 24 to get **4:5**.
9	**5:3:4**	Mario's age: $15 \times {}^3/_5 = 9$ Asha's age: 15 × 80% = 15 × 0.8 = 12 Therefore, the ratio of John's to Mario's to Asha's ages is 15:9:12 = **5:3:4**.
10	**20%**	1 hour = 60 minutes Duration of adverts: 60min − 48min = 12min Therefore, the proportion of time spent watching adverts is 12 ÷ 60 × 100 = **20%**.
11	**98l**	1min 10sec = 60sec + 10sec = 70sec 70sec ÷ 20sec = 3.5 Therefore, the amount of water that will escape is 28l × 3.5 = **98l**.
12	**39**	Number of shapes in pattern: 11 Number of full patterns: 144 ÷ 11 = 13 R 1 → 1 remaining shape (square) There are 3 triangles in a single pattern. Therefore, the number of triangles is 13 × 3 = **39**.
13	**238**	The ratio of staff to customers is 3:14. 3:14 is equivalent to 42:C (where C represents the number of customers). 42 ÷ 3 = 14 so C = 14 × 14 = 196. Therefore, the total number of people is 42 + 196 = **238**.
14	**12.75km**	As the scale is 1:150000, the real distance of the line is 8.5cm × 150000 = 0.085m × 150000 = 12750m. 1000m = 1km, therefore 12750m = **12.75km**.
15	**1:250000**	12.5cm = 0.125m and 31.25km = 31250m. 31250m ÷ 0.125m = 250000 Therefore, the scale is **1:250000**.

Question	Answer	Explanation
1	1	$x + 5 = 6$ Subtract 5 from both sides. Therefore, $x = 6 - 5 = $ **1**.
2	6	$3a = 18$ Divide both sides by 3. Therefore, $a = 18 \div 3 = $ **6**.
3	2	$x \times x \times x = x^3 = 8$ Cube root both sides. Therefore, $x = \sqrt[3]{8} = $ **2**.
4	6	Substitute in $z = 5$ and $y = 2$. Therefore, $2(5 - 2) = 2 \times 3 = $ **6**.
5	b^2	Area of square = length × width Therefore, the expression is $b \times b = b^2$.
6	20	$x \div 4 = 5$ Multiply both sides by 4. $x = 4 \times 5$ Therefore, $x = $ **20**.
7	£31.50	$x \div 3 = £10.50$ Multiply both sides by 3. Therefore, $x = £10.50 \times 3 = $ **£31.50**.
8	123.4	$1234x = 1234 \times x$ Substitute in $x = 0.1$. Therefore, $1234 \times 0.1 = $ **123.4**.
9	2	$4c - 14 = -3c$ Subtract 4c from both sides. $-14 = -3c - 4c = -7c$ Divide both sides by −7. Therefore, $c = -14 \div -7 = $ **2**.
10	0	$y = 12 - 3x$ Substitute in $x = 4$. Therefore, $y = 12 - (3 \times 4) = 12 - 12 = $ **0**.
11	4	Working forwards from the input, $(10 \div 2) - 1 = 5 - 1 = $ **4**.
12	72	Working forwards from the input, $6 \times 12 = $ **72**.
13	14	Working backwards from the output, $(60 \div 10) + 8 = 6 + 8 = $ **14**.
14	0	Working forwards from the input, $(189 + 23) \times 0 = 212 \times 0 = $ **0**.
15	−16	Working forwards from the input, $16 - (2 \times 16) = 16 - 32 = $ **−16**.

Question	Answer	Explanation
1	**63**	$x \div 3 - 9 = 12$ Add 9 to both sides. $x \div 3 = 12 + 9 = 21$ Multiply both sides by 3. Therefore, $x = 21 \times 3 = $ **63**.
2	**14**	Lin is 21 years old. Emma is 2 years younger than Lin, so she is 19 years old. Emma is 5 years older than Hiten. Therefore, Hiten is $19 - 5 = $ **14** years old.
3	**12**	$3y + 18 = 54$ Subtract 18 from both sides. $3y = 54 - 18 = 36$ Divide both sides by 3. Therefore, $y = 36 \div 3 = $ **12**.
4	**1.25**	Substitute in $p = 0.5$ and $q = 1.5$. $0.5(3 \times 1.5 - 4 \times 0.5) = 0.5(4.5 - 2) = 0.5 \times 2.5 = $ **1.25**
5	**2(2x + 3)**	Perimeter of the rectangle: $2x + 2(x + 3) = 2x + 2x + 6 = 4x + 6 = $ **2(2x + 3)**
6	**−6**	$14b + 23 = 8b - 13$ Subtract $8b$ from both sides. $14b - 8b + 23 = 6b + 23 = -13$ Subtract 23 from both sides. $6b = -13 - 23 = -36$ Divide both sides by 6. Therefore, $b = -36 \div 6 = $ **−6**.
7	**£6.55**	Ann will receive £14.80 − (£3.40 + £4.85) = £14.80 − £8.25 = **£6.55**.
8	**4cm**	Space taken up by gaps: 20cm × 4 = 80cm Combined height of the 5 pieces of wood: 100cm − 80cm = 20cm Therefore, the height of each shelf is 20cm ÷ 5 = **4cm**.
9	**8**	$3t + 2s = 37$ Substitute in $t = 7$. $(3 \times 7) + 2s = 21 + 2s = 37$ Subtract 21 from both sides. $2s = 37 - 21 = 16$ Therefore, $s = 16 \div 2 = $ **8**.
10	**6**	Substitute in $x = -1$. $3w - w = 4(2 - (-1)) = 4(2 + 1) = 4(3) = 12$ $2w = 12$ Therefore, $w = 12 \div 2 = $ **6**.
11	**143**	Working forwards from the input, $(4 + 9) \times 11 = 13 \times 11 = $ **143**.
12	**4.5**	Working forwards from the input, $(^1/_4 - ^1/_5) \times 90 = (0.25 - 0.2) \times 90 = 0.05 \times 90 = $ **4.5**.
13	**20**	Working backwards from the output, $((100 \div 5) - 15) \times 4 = (20 - 15) \times 4 = 5 \times 4 = $ **20**.
14	**19**	Working forwards from the input, $(35 - 3^3) + \sqrt{121} = (35 - 27) + 11 = 8 + 11 = $ **19**.
15	**35**	$18 + \text{Input } 2 = 53$ Therefore, Input 2 is $53 - 18 = $ **35**.

Question	Answer	Explanation
1	$4s + 2t$	The two missing side lengths are $t - u$ (shorter side) and $2s - b$. Therefore, the perimeter is $t + 2s + u + b + (t - u) + (2s - b) = \mathbf{4s + 2t}$.
2	**1.19**	Substitute in $a = 0.75$, $b = 0.65$ and $c = 0.25$. Therefore, $z = (2 \times 0.75 - 0.65)(0.65 + 3 \times 0.25) = (1.5 - 0.65)(0.65 + 0.75) = 0.85 \times 1.4 = \mathbf{1.19}$.
3	$2(5n - 8)$	$((n \times 5) - 8) \times 2 = \mathbf{2(5n - 8)}$ OR $\mathbf{10n - 16}$
4	**1.5**	$41x - 197 = 34 - 113x$ Add $113x$ to both sides. $41x + 113x - 197 = 154x - 197 = 34$ Add 197 to both sides. $154x = 34 + 197 = 231$ Therefore, $x = 231 \div 154 = \mathbf{1.5}$.
5	**£49.35**	Amount daughter received: $x \times \frac{2}{3} = £70.50$ $x = £70.50 \div \frac{2}{3} = £70.50 \times \frac{3}{2} = £70.50 \times 1.5 = £105.75$ Amount niece received: $£105.75 \times \frac{1}{5} = £105.75 \div 5 = £21.15$ Therefore, the difference is $£70.50 - £21.15 = \mathbf{£49.35}$.
6	**3**	$((10 + 3^2) - ?) \times 5.5 = ((10 + 9) - ?) \times 5.5 = 5.5(19 - ?) = 88$ $88 \div 5.5 = 16 = 19 - ?$ Therefore, the missing number is $19 - 16 = \mathbf{3}$.
7	**100**	$(17 \times 7) - (327 \div 3) = 119 - 109 = 10 = \frac{P}{10}$ Therefore, $P = 10 \times 10 = \mathbf{100}$.
8	$\mathbf{\frac{19}{7}}$	$\frac{7}{8}y - 1\frac{5}{8} = \frac{7}{8}y - \frac{13}{8} = \frac{3}{4}$ Add $\frac{13}{8}$ to both sides. $\frac{7}{8}y = \frac{3}{4} + \frac{13}{8} = \frac{6}{8} + \frac{13}{8} = \frac{19}{8}$ Therefore, $y = \frac{19}{8} \div \frac{7}{8} = \frac{19}{8} \times \frac{8}{7} = 19 \times \frac{1}{7} = \mathbf{\frac{19}{7}}$.
9	**53.6**	$1340 + 1340 + 1340 + 1340 = 1340 \times 4 = 5360$ $5360 \div 100 = \mathbf{53.6}$
10	**40**	Working backwards from the output, $((105 \div 7) + 5) \times 2 = (15 + 5) \times 2 = 20 \times 2 = \mathbf{40}$.
11	$c^2 - b^2$	As shown in the diagram, you can form two squares. The area of the L shape can be expressed by taking the area of the smaller square ($b \times b = b^2$) from that of the larger square ($c \times c = c^2$). Therefore, the area is $\mathbf{c^2 - b^2}$.
12	**−6**	$(2x)^2 = 144$ $2x = \sqrt{144} = 12$ or -12 As we are told we are looking for a negative number, $x = -12 \div 2 = \mathbf{-6}$.
13	**12.36**	Working forwards from the input, $((2.65 + 3.37) \times 2.5) - 2.69 = (6.02 \times 2.5) - 2.69 = 15.05 - 2.69 = \mathbf{12.36}$.
14	$2(2a + b + c)$	Perimeter of the shape: $(4 \times a) + (2 \times b) + (2 \times c) = 4a + 2b + 2c = \mathbf{2(2a + b + c)}$
15	**88.7**	Working forwards from the input, $((825 + 167) \div 10) - 10.5 = (992 \div 10) - 10.5 = 99.2 - 10.5 = \mathbf{88.7}$.

Chapter 7: Averages and Representing Data - Beginner

Question	Answer	Explanation
1	2	Mean = Sum of numbers ÷ Amount of numbers Therefore, the average is 8 ÷ 4 = **2**.
2	20%	The mode score is the score which occurs with the highest frequency, which is **20%** as it occurs 3 times.
3	16	Sum of numbers: 27 + 11 + 15 + 13 + 3 + 15 + 28 = 112 Therefore, the mean is 112 ÷ 7 = **16**.
4	15	Counters in ascending order: 3, 11, 13, 15, 15, 27, 28 There are 7 values in total. 7 is an odd number so the median number is the 4th value. Therefore, the median is **15**.
5	15	The mode is **15** as it is the most frequently occurring number (2 times).
6	25	Range: highest value – lowest value Therefore, the range is 28 – 3 = **25**.
7	12	Number of CDs in ascending order: 9, 11, 12, 14, 19 There are 5 values in total. 5 is an odd number so the median number is the 3rd value. Therefore, the median is **12**.
8	8km	(11km + 2km + 14km + 8km + 5km) ÷ 5 = 40km ÷ 5 = **8km**
9	6	The pie chart shows that a quarter had no pets. Therefore, the number of people with no pets is 24 ÷ 4 = **6**.
10	5km/h	Average speed (km/h) = distance travelled (km) ÷ time (h) 10km ÷ 120min = 10km ÷ 2h = **5km/h**
11	3	**3** people have a score higher than 10.
12	16	**16** people selected blue as their favourite colour.
13	28	13 + 5 + 8 + 2 = **28**
14	50%	Number of days with temperature below 15°C: 3 Total number of days: 6 Therefore, the percentage is $^3/_6 \times 100 = ^1/_2 \times 100$ = **50%**.
15	51	Number of detached houses sold: 15 Numbers of flats sold: 36 Therefore, the combined number sold is 15 + 36 = **51**.

Question	Answer	Explanation
1	8	Sum of scores: 13 + 8 + 1 + 20 + 15 + 16 + 10 + 17 + X = 100 + X (100 + X) ÷ 9 = 12 Therefore, the 9th person's score is (9 × 12) – 100 = 108 – 100 = **8**.
2	1.3cm	Range: highest value – lowest value Therefore, the range is 4.2cm – 2.9cm = **1.3cm**.
3	1°C	(2°C + (–1°C) + (–1°C) + 2°C + 3°C + (–1°C) + 3°C) ÷ 7 = 7°C ÷ 7 = **1°C**
4	2°C	Temperatures in ascending order: –1°C, –1°C, –1°C, 2°C, 2°C, 3°C, 3°C There are 7 values in total. 7 is an odd number so the median number is the 4th value. Therefore, the median is **2°C**.
5	–1°C	The mode is **–1°C** as it is the most frequently occurring number (3 times).
6	4°C	Range: highest value – lowest value Therefore, the range is 3°C – (–1°C) = **4°C**.
7	£0.90	Total price of toothbrushes: £21.50 – (£2.00 + £16.80) = £21.50 – £18.80 = £2.70 Therefore, the price of one toothbrush is £2.70 ÷ 3 = **£0.90**.
8	44	Total number of people: 14 + 9 + 3 + 4 + 13 + 8 + 7 = 58 Number of people who had only been to England: 14 Therefore, the number of people is 58 – 14 = **44**.
9	$^4/_{17}$	Total number of people: 14 + 12 + 5 + 3 = 34 Number of people who own more than one car: 5 + 3 = 8 Therefore, the fraction of people who own more than one car is $^8/_{34}$ = **$^4/_{17}$**.
10	1,150	Number of weekend visitors: (200 × 7) + (200 × $^1/_2$) = 1400 + 100 = 1500 Number of Friday visitors: 200 + (200 × $^1/_2$) + (200 × $^1/_4$) = 200 + 100 + 50 = 350 Therefore, the difference in visitors is 1500 – 350 = **1150**.
11	60	360° – (90° + 45°) = 360° – 135° = 225° Therefore, the number of children that walked is $^{225°}/_{360°}$ × 96 = **60**.
12	40%	For each student, the bar with the greater length represents the higher result. Number of pupils with higher English result: 2 Therefore, the percentage of pupils is $^2/_5$ × 100 = **40%**.
13	25g	Convert all values to g: 0.25kg = 250g, 25000mg = 25g, 0.025kg = 25g Three values out of five are equivalent to **25g**, therefore that is the mode value.
14	57.5km/h	(50km/h + 65km/h) ÷ 2 = 115km/h ÷ 2 = **57.5km/h**
15	8°C	Mean temperature: (20°C + 25°C + 15°C + 30°C + 35°C + 25°C) ÷ 6 = 150°C ÷ 6 = 25°C Therefore, the difference is 33°C – 25°C = **8°C**.

Question	Answer	Explanation
1	6	If the largest number is 17 and the range is 20, then the set must consist of 17 − 20 = −3. The final two numbers must be 5 because that is the mode. Therefore, the mean is (17 + (−3) + 5 + 5) ÷ 4 = 24 ÷ 4 = **6**.
2	$^8/_{13}$	Missing value: 29 − (14 + 4 + 5) = 6 Total number of children: 18 + 4 + 14 + 6 + 5 + 6 + 12 = 65. Children with yellow or purple but not both: 18 + 4 + 12 + 6 = 40 Therefore, the fraction of children is $^{40}/_{65}$ = $^8/_{13}$.
3	4,000ml	Amount of petrol used: 18l Average: 18l ÷ 5 = 3.6l = 3600ml 3600ml rounded to the nearest thousand millilitres is **4000ml**.
4	17	From the information given we can identify the following numbers: 30, 25, 25, 42. If 30 is the median and 42 is the largest number, the missing value must be between 30 and 42. This makes 25 the smallest number. Therefore, the range is 42 − 25 = **17**.
5	£18.30	When the distance is 2.5 miles, the taxi fare is £15. £15 × 22% = £15 × 0.22 = £3.30 Therefore, Trevor paid £15 + £3.30 = **£18.30**.
6	0.87	2:2:4 = 1:1:2 Sum of ratio parts: 1 + 1 + 2 = 4 3.48 ÷ 4 = 0.87 Therefore, the mode value is 0.87 × 1 = **0.87**.
7	126	Carrots: $^{120°}/_{360°}$ × 432 = $^1/_3$ × 432 = 144 Cabbage: $^{360° − (90° + 45° + 90° + 120°)}/_{360°}$ × 432 = $^{15°}/_{360°}$ × 432 = $^1/_{24}$ × 432 = 18 Therefore, the difference is 144 − 18 = **126**.
8	Friday	$3^3 − √64 − 1^{10}$ = 27 − 8 − 1 = 18 18°C − 8°C = 10°C → **Friday**
9	5.5	(6 + 8 + 4 + 9 + 1 + 5) ÷ 6 = 33 ÷ 6 = **5.5**
10	6	(6 + 8 + 4 + 9 + 1 + 5 + 5 + 3 + 10 + 8 + 9 + 4) ÷ 12 = 72 ÷ 12 = **6**
11	9	Range: highest value − lowest value Therefore, the range is 10 − 1 = **9**.
12	5.5	Scores in numerical order: 1, 3, 4, 4, 5, 5, 6, 8, 8, 9, 9, 10 There are 12 values in total. 12 is an even number so the median mark is the mean of the 6th and 7th value (middle values). Therefore, the median is (5 + 6) ÷ 2 = **5.5**.
13	$^5/_{12}$	Average: 6 (see question 10) Number of scores above average: 5 (8, 8, 9, 9, 10) Therefore, the fraction of students who scored above average is $^5/_{12}$.
14	180	Mean: (5 + 6 + 7 + 1 + 6) ÷ 5 = 25 ÷ 5 = 5 Range: 7 − 1 = 6 Mode: 6 Therefore, the product is 5 × 6 × 6 = **180**.
15	0.2m	(10cm + 110cm + 40cm + 90cm + ?cm + 100cm + 50cm) ÷ 7 = (400cm + ?) ÷ 7 = 600mm = 60cm Therefore, the length of stone 5 is (60cm × 7) − 400cm = 420cm − 400cm = 20cm = **0.2m**.

Question	Answer	Explanation
1	**80mm**	1cm = 10mm → 8cm × 10 = **80mm**
2	**9,500g**	1kg = 1000g → 9.5kg × 1000 = **9500g**
3	**2l**	1000ml = 1l → 2000ml ÷ 1000 = **2l**
4	**1.05m**	1.21m – 16cm = 1.21m – 0.16m = **1.05m**
5	**32**	1 gallon = 8 pints = 16 half-pints → 2 gallons = 16 × 2 = **32**
6	**7 miles**	1 mile ≈ 2km Therefore, 10km ≈ 5 miles. 5 miles + 2 miles = **7 miles**
7	**12°C**	The scale goes up in divisions of 1°C. The thermometer shows a temperature of 2 points above 10°C which is equal to 10°C + 2°C = **12°C**.
8	**750ml**	The scale goes up in divisions of 0.25l. The liquid line shows a volume of 1 point above 0.5l which is equal to 0.5l + 0.25l = 0.75l = **750ml**.
9	**10m**	As the scale is 1:200, 5cm on the map represents a distance of 5cm × 200 = 1000cm = **10m**.
10	**4.3cm**	The scale goes up in divisions of 0.2cm. The arrow points between 4.2 and 4.4, which is equal to **4.3cm**.
11	**3.5cm**	As the scale is 1:300, 10.5m is drawn with a length of 10.5m ÷ 300 = 1050cm ÷ 300 = **3.5cm**.
12	**800g**	The scale goes up in divisions of 0.2kg. The arrow is at the first point after 1.0kg, which is equal to 1.2kg. 2kg – 1.2kg = 0.8kg = **800g**
13	**5°C**	3°C – (−2°C) = 3°C + 2°C = **5°C**
14	**16**	Volume of water in jug: 0.8l = 800ml 800ml ÷ 50ml = **16**
15	**145mm**	Values in centimetres (given order): 1.9cm, 2.2cm, 9cm , 0.65cm, 6cm, 14.5cm The largest value is 14.5cm, therefore the answer is **145mm**.

Question	Answer	Explanation
1	**20m**	2500cm ÷ 100 = 25m 0.005km × 1000 = 5m Therefore, the difference is 25m − 5m = **20m**.
2	**9.035kg**	3627g ÷ 1000 = 3.627kg 5.408kg + 3.627kg = **9.035kg**
3	**£12.00**	6 × £1 = £6 = 2 ounces 4 ounces ÷ 2 ounces = 2 Therefore, 4 ounces is £6 × 2 = **£12**.
4	**600ml**	Beaker A: 1.5l × $^1/_5$ = 1500ml × $^1/_5$ = 300ml Beaker B: 1500ml × 60% = 1500ml × 0.6 = 900ml Therefore, the average is (300ml + 900ml) ÷ 2 = **600ml**.
5	**16 inches**	6 foot 2 inches = (12 inches × 6) + 2 inches = 74 inches 90 inches − 74 inches = **16 inches**
6	**£8.00**	10.4 Euros ÷ 1.3 Euros = 8 £1 × 8 = **£8.00**
7	**0.2**	The scale goes up in divisions of 0.025. Left arrow: 4.725, Right Arrow: 4.925 Therefore, the difference is 4.925 − 4.725 = **0.2**.
8	**15°C**	Temperature on thermometer: −13°C −13°C − (−28°C) = **15°C**
9	**£1.89**	Weight of apples: 3.5kg 54p × 3.5 = 189p = **£1.89**
10	**20cm**	360m = 36000cm 36000cm ÷ 1800 = **20cm**
11	**3.6cm**	Side length: 1.7cm − 0.8cm = 0.9cm Therefore, the perimeter is 0.9cm × 4 = **3.6cm**.
12	**6,350g**	The scale goes up in divisions of 0.2kg. A = 12.7kg ÷ 2 = 6.35kg **6350g**
13	**$^1/_2$ pint OR 0.5 pints**	1.5l − 1.25l = 0.25l = 250ml 1 pint = 500ml 500ml ÷ 250ml = 2, therefore 250ml is 1 pint ÷ 2 = $^1/_2$ **pint OR 0.5 pints**.
14	**5.13kg**	2850g × 80% = 2850g × 0.8 = 2280g 2850g + 2280g = 5130g = **5.13kg**
15	**4.55m**	3.5cm × 260 = 910cm 910cm ÷ 2 = 455cm = **4.55m**

Question	Answer	Explanation
1	237,000g	901kg + 9kg + 527kg = 1437kg 1 tonne = 1000kg so 1.2 tonnes = 1.2 × 1000kg = 1200kg 1437kg – 1200kg = 237kg = **237000g**
2	35,200 yards	$1\,^2/_3$ hr = 60min + $(60 × \,^2/_3)$min = 60min + 40min = 100min At 100min, the distance is 20 miles. 1760 yards × 20 = **35200 yards**
3	1.06l	Amount of water in container at start: 2l × 78% = 2000ml × 0.78 = 1560ml Amount of water lost = 50ml × 10 = 500ml Therefore, the amount of water left is 1560ml – 500ml = 1060ml = **1.06l.**
4	1,080m	√81mm = 9mm 9mm × 30000 = 270000mm = 270m 270m × 4 = **1080m**
5	28,800mm²	24cm ÷ 2 = 12cm 24cm × 12cm = 240mm × 120mm = **28800mm²**
6	£1.00	55p × 12 = 660p = £6.60 and £1.10 × 4 = £4.40 250ml × 12 = 3000ml = 3l and 2l × 4 = 8l 3l + 8l = 11l £6.60 + £4.40 = £11.00 £11.00 ÷ 11 = **£1.00**
7	28.75cm	12.346cm + 148mm + $1\,^3/_5$ cm = 12.346cm + 14.8cm + 1.6cm = 28.746cm The number 6 (thousandths column) is $\geq$ 5 so the number 4 (hundredths column) is rounded up to 5 giving **28.75cm** to two decimal places.
8	0.02km	100cm = 1m → 2000cm = 20m 1000m = 1km → 20m = **0.02km**
9	9	Capacity of container: 4l × 0.9 = 3.6l Amount of liquid in jug: 0.4l 3.6l ÷ 0.4l = **9**
10	9m	Guwon: 90m Songyo: 3240 inches = (3240 × 2.5)cm = 8100cm = 81m 90m – 81m = **9m**
11	97	1.75m = 175cm 18mm = 1.8cm 175cm ÷ 1.8cm = 97.2222... → **97** coins
12	1,920 ounces	Weight of 3 sticks: 1 stone 6 pounds = 14 pounds + 6 pounds = 20 pounds = 16 ounces × 20 = 320 ounces Therefore, the weight of 18 sticks is 320 ounces × 6 = **1920 ounces.**
13	2,520g	X:Y:Z = 1:3:1 Sum of ratio parts: 1 + 3 + 1 = 5 12.6kg ÷ 5 = 2.52kg 2.52kg × 1 = 2.52kg = **2520g**
14	220 miles	(30km + 25km + 50km + 60km + 55km) × 2 = 440km 440km ÷ 2 = **220 miles**
15	1,160 ounces	1000kg = 1 tonne → 0.029 tonnes = (1000 × 0.029)kg = 29kg = 29000g 29000g ÷ 25 = **1160 ounces**

Question	Answer	Explanation
1	30	There are **30** days in the month of June.
2	Sunday	If the 10th is a Thursday, the 17th is also a Thursday. Therefore, the 20th would be a **Sunday**.
3	6	She has **6** days: 25th, 26th, 27th, 28th, 29th, 30th
4	29th April	The date will be two weeks from the 15th. 15th + 14 days → 29th Therefore, the date is **29th April**.
5	4	The next Monday would be the 10th of August, then the 17th, then the 24th, and then the 31st. Therefore, there will be **4** more magazines published in August.
6	12hr	A day is split evenly between "am" and "pm". There are 24 hours in a day, therefore "pm" lasts for **12 hours**.
7	360sec	1 minute = 60 seconds 60 × 6sec = **360sec**
8	9.45am	The hour hand is between 9 and 10 and the minute hand is on 9. 9 × 5min = 45min Therefore, the time shown is **9.45am**.
9	10.50pm	11.45pm – 55 minutes → **10.50pm**
10	21:15	9.00pm is the twenty-first hour in the day. A quarter of an hour is equal to 15 minutes. Therefore, the 24-hour time is **21:15**.
11	12.18am	00:18 is the first hour in the day. Therefore, the 12-hour time is **12.18am**.
12	80min	11:59 to 12:59 → 1hr = 60min 12:59 to 13:19 → 20min 60min + 20min = **80min**
13	12:55	The difference between 10:45 and 11:55 is 70 minutes. Therefore, boat C will arrive at Greenwich 70 minutes after 11:45 → **12:55**.
14	110min	11:53 to 13:53 → 2hr The train reaches Oxford at 13:43 which is 10 minutes before 13:53. Therefore, the duration of the journey is 2hr – 10min = 120min – 10min = **110min**.
15	20:33	19:21 to 19:47 → 26min 26min + 20min + 26min = 72min 19:21 + 72min → **20:33**

Chapter 9: Dates, Times and Timetables - Intermediate

Question	Answer	Explanation
1	92	October + November + December = 31 + 30 + 31 = **92**
2	$^4/_{15}$	Saturdays: 6th, 13th, 20th, 27th Sundays: 7th, 14th, 21st, 28th Therefore, the fraction of days that are weekends is $^8/_{30}$ = $^4/_{15}$.
3	Tuesday	Days in July: Saturday 27th + 4 days → Wednesday 31st July Days in August: Thursday 1st August + 5 days → **Tuesday** 6th August
4	4th May	120hr ÷ 24 = 5 days 29th April + 5 days → **4th May**
5	7	Leap years occur every 4 years as does the date 29th February. Inclusive of 1992 and 2016, the following **7** years were leap years; 1992, 1996, 2000, 2004, 2008, 2012 and 2016.
6	6	Clock B is 2 minutes faster than clock A → 2 × 60sec = 120sec Therefore, the number of days clock B has gained is 120 ÷ 20 = **6** days.
7	143min	21:14 (9.14pm) to 11.37pm → 2hr 23min = 60min + 60min + 23min = **143min**
8	21:00	70min + 60min + 20min = 150min = 2hr 30min 2hr 30min after 18:30 is **21:00**.
9	4.05pm	60min × $^2/_3$ = 40min 40min before 4.45pm is **4.05pm**.
10	73min	Planned start time: 4min before 10:02 is 09:58. Planned arrival time: 120sec (2min) after 11:09 is 11:11. Therefore, the journey time from 09:58 to 11:11 is 1hr 13min = **73min**.
11	9hr	Left clock: 6.45am Right clock: 4.10pm The number of full hours between both times is **9hr**.
12	231min	Pierre caught the 12:33 train and arrived in Bath at 15:29. He left Bath at 19:20. Therefore, he was in Bath for 3hr 51min = **231min**.
13	Rodmell	The bus leaves Peacehaven at 07:17. After 34 minutes the time is 07:51. At this time the next stop for the bus (**Rodmell**) is at 07:53.
14	Drez	The train was stationary at Allex for 1 minute, Blex for 2 minutes, Cloud for 8 minutes, Drez for 6 minutes and Epex for 3 minutes. The second longest duration was **Drez** at 6 minutes.
15	90hr	1 day = 24 hours 3.75 × 24hr = **90hr**

Question	Answer	Explanation
1	3	Odd numbered months (January, March, May, July, September and November): 31 + 31 + 31 + 31 + 30 + 30 = 184 Even numbered months (February, April, June, August, October and December): 28 + 30 + 30 + 31 + 31 + 31 = 181 Therefore, the difference between these is 184 − 181 = **3**.
2	225min	22:49 on Saturday is 1hr 11min before 00:00 on Sunday. 02:34 is 2hr 34min after 00:00 on Sunday. Therefore, the length between the times is 1hr 11min + 2hr 34min = 3hr 45min = (60 × 3 + 45)min = **225min**.
3	218 minutes before midnight	The time on the clock is 8.20pm. The first time in the table is 20:03, which is 8.03pm and is 17 minutes short of 8.20pm. The second time is 11.20pm, which is further away from 8.20pm than 20:03. The third time is 8.22pm, which is only 2 minutes off 8.20pm and is the closest so far. The fourth time is 8.48pm and the fifth time is 8.42pm. The closest time to 8.20pm is therefore 8.22pm (**218 minutes before midnight**).
4	12.33pm	35min + 42min + 1.9hr + 420sec + 15min = (35 + 42 + 114 + 7 + 15)min = 213min = 3hr 33min 3hr 33min after 9.00am is **12.33pm**.
5	Thursday	Mrs Patel left on Thursday 28th June. The following Thursdays are 7 days apart. Thus the 5th July, 12th July, 19th July, 26th July and 2nd August are Thursdays. Therefore, 2nd August is a **Thursday**.
6	Train 3	Train 1 took 56 minutes, train 2 took 43 minutes, train 3 took 48 minutes, train 4 took 46 minutes and train 5 took 67 minutes. Therefore, the third fastest train was **train 3**.
7	75%	Three of the four months (January, June, July and December) have 31 days, which is $\frac{3}{4} \times 100$ = **75%**.
8	£17.00	Two of the times were less than $\sqrt{121}$ = 11 seconds, so he receives 2 × £4 = £8 for these. Three of the times are less than $(2^4 - 2^0)$ = 16 − 1 = 15sec, so he receives 3 × £3 = £9 for these. Therefore, the total amount he receives is £8 + £9 = **£17**.
9	7hr	$3\frac{7}{8}$ days = (3 × 24) + ($\frac{7}{8}$ × 24) = 72 + 21 = 93hr 100hr − 93hr = **7hr**
10	12th November	November has 30 days. A sixth of 30 days is 5 days. 5 days before 16th (inclusive of this date) is **12th November**.
11	33.5hr	Monday: 8hr 35min, Tuesday: 8hr 20min, Wednesday: 8hr 5min, Thursday: 6hr 30min, Friday: 7hr This is a total of 38.5 hours. However, he also took 5 hours for lunches, so he actually worked 38.5hr − 5hr = **33.5hr**.
12	104	2 years = 2 × 365 days = 730 days 730 ÷ 7 = **104** weeks
13	15:50	45min + ($\frac{1}{3}$ × 45min) + 15min = 45min + 15min + 15min = 75min = 1hr 15min 1hr 15min after 14:35 is **15:50**.
14	Wednesday 7th at 12.00pm	A week is 7 days or 7 × 24 = 168hr. Halfway through this is 168hr ÷ 2 = 84hr = 3 days 12hr. 3 days 12hr after 00:00 on Sunday 4th is **Wednesday 7th at 12.00pm**.
15	45min	Kriti waits between 11:01 and 11:46, which is **45 minutes**.

Chapter 10: Lines, Angles and Bearings - Beginner

Question	Answer	Explanation
1	T	A vertical line is one that goes from top to bottom. It is at right angles to a horizontal line. **T** is a vertical line.
2	**5.6cm**	Perpendicular lines are lines that are at right-angles (90°) to each other. Line E is perpendicular to line D and has a length of **5.6cm**.
3	**360°**	The exterior angles of any hexagon sum to **360°**.
4	**180°**	The interior angles of any triangle sum to **180°**.
5	**65°**	Angles in a right-angle sum to 90°. $q = 90° - 25° = \mathbf{65°}$
6	**reflex**	Angles greater than 180° are called **reflex** angles.
7	**30°**	Angles in a circle sum to 360°. $360° \div 12 = \mathbf{30°}$
8	**110°**	Angles in a quadrilateral sum to 360°. $x = 360° - (90° + 90° + 70°) = 360° - 250° = \mathbf{110°}$
9	**100°**	Angles on a straight line sum to 180°. $y = 180° - (45° + 35°) = 180° - 80° = \mathbf{100°}$
10	**45°**	An acute angle is an angle less than 90°. The only angle less than 90° in the list is **45°**.
11	**108°**	The interior angles in a regular pentagon sum to 540°. $c = 540° \div 5 = \mathbf{108°}$
12	**north**	On a compass, **north** is directly opposite south.
13	**east and west**	On a compass, **east and west** are both 90° from south.
14	**D**	The post box is directly west of the building in diagram **D**.
15	**P**	Point **P** is north-west of point S.

Question	Answer	Explanation
1	**30°**	The angles in an equilateral triangle are each 60° and the smaller angle between two perpendicular lines is 90°. 90° – 60° = **30°**
2	**4cm**	4 of the lines are parallel. Average length: (6cm + 4cm + 3cm + 3cm) ÷ 4 = 16cm ÷ 4 = **4cm**
3	**7cm**	Longest diagonal: 20cm Therefore, the length of the shortest diagonal is 20cm × 35% = 20cm × 0.35 = **7cm**.
4	**scalene**	Angles in a triangle sum to 180˚ so the third angle is 180° – (35° + 78°) = 180° – 113° = 67°. All three angles are different, therefore it must be a **scalene** triangle. ***Acute angled triangle*** also acceptable.
5	**33.75°**	$^3/_8 \times 90° = $ **33.75°**
6	**82°**	Angles around a point sum to 360°. R = 360° – (90° + 121° + 67°) = 360° – 278° = **82°**
7	**95°**	The kite has two equal angles which are opposite each other. Therefore, X + X + 105° + 65° = 2X + 170° = 360°. 2X = 360° – 170° = 190° X = 190° ÷ 2 = **95°**
8	**49°**	If the largest angle in a triangle is 130°, the remaining two angles must sum to 180° – 130° = 50°. If angles can only be measured to the nearest whole number of degrees, the smallest possible angle would be 1°, meaning that the second largest angle would be **49°**.
9	**68°**	A parallelogram has two equal and also opposite angles. Therefore, Y + Y + 112° + 112° = 2Y + 224° = 360°. 2Y = 360° – 224° = 136° Y = 136° ÷ 2 = **68°**
10	**10.00pm**	If the hour hand turns through 120˚, which is $^{120}/_{360} = ^1/_3$ of a clockwise turn from 6.00pm, the new time will be $^1/_3 \times 12$hr = 4 hr on from 6.00pm → **10.00pm**.
11	**270°**	The interior angles of a regular octagon sum to 1080°. Each angle therefore measures 1080° ÷ 8 = 135°. Therefore, the sum of angles C and D is 135° + 135° = **270°**.
12	**135°**	The anticlockwise turn from south-west to east on a compass is 45° + 90° = **135°**.
13	**south-west**	315° clockwise from west is **south-west**.
14	**south-east**	The largest prime number on the grid is 23, which is **south-east** of the grey square.
15	**north-west**	Billy is at the park as the school is directly north of him and the shop is west of him. Therefore, the post office is **north-west** of Billy.

Question	Answer	Explanation
1	**2°**	In an acute-angle triangle, the interior angles are all less than 90°, which means the two largest angles could be 89° and 89°. Therefore, the smallest angle is 180° − (89° + 89°) = 180° − 178° = **2°**.
2	**13.8**	Sides 4 and 6 are perpendicular to side 5. 4 + 6 = 10 $10^2 = 100$ 113.8 − 100 = **13.8**
3	**45°**	As the angle between any two adjacent hour times is 30°, angle A = 1.5 × 30° = **45°**.
4	**24°**	Sum of ratio parts: 2 + 10 + 3 = 15 As angles in a triangle add up to 180°, each part is worth 180° ÷ 15 = 12°. Therefore, the smallest angle is 2 × 12° = **24°**.
5	**10mm**	Side length: 132cm ÷ 8 = 16.5cm 4 of the 8 sides are either horizontal or vertical so the sum of these sides is 4 × 16.5cm = 66cm = 660mm. Therefore, the difference is 660mm − 650mm = **10mm**.
6	**82.6°**	Angle b = 180° − (41.3° + 90°) = 180° − 131.3° = 48.7° Angle a = 360° − (48.7° + 90° + 90°) = 360° − 228.7° = 131.3° Therefore, angle a − angle b is 131.3° − 48.7° = **82.6°**.
7	**112.5°**	Angles in a triangle add up to 180°. $q + 2q + 5q = 8q = 180°$ $q = 180° ÷ 8 = 22.5°$ Therefore, the largest angle is 5 × q = 5 × 22.5° = **112.5°**.
8	**743.25°**	Reflex angles are greater than 180°. Therefore, the sum of these is 341.72° + 181.97° + 219.56° = **743.25°**.
9	**202.5°**	$\frac{3}{4} × (90° × 3) = \frac{3}{4} × 270° = $ **202.5°**
10	**53.6°**	Angles on a straight line sum to 180°. Q = 180° − (24.1° + 52.9° + 49.4°) = 180° − 126.4° = **53.6°**
11	**C**	Imagine walking from the start square: **forward 3, turn left 90°, forward 3, turn right 90°, forward 4**.
12	**4**	West of the number 7 on a clock face is 90° anticlockwise, which is the number **4**.
13	**30°**	Interior angles of a regular hexagon sum to 720°. Each interior angle: 720° ÷ 6 = 120° Therefore, X is 120° − 90° = **30°**.
14	**east**	Albert is north of Marta meaning that Albert is either at points 1 or 2. Jess is east of Marta, meaning that she must be at point 5, Marta must be at point 4 and Albert at point 1. Alan is at point 2. Sophie is therefore at point 3, which is **east** of the library.
15	**90°**	The turn from south-west to north-west is $\frac{2}{8}$ of a circle = $\frac{2}{8} × 360° = \frac{1}{4} × 360° =$ **90°**.

Question	Answer	Explanation
1	pentagon	A five-sided shape is called a **pentagon**.
2	equilateral	A triangle with all sides equal is called an **equilateral** triangle.
3	2	A parallelogram has **2** pairs of parallel lines.
4	9cm	Opposite sides of a rectangle are equal in length. Therefore, the length of Y is **9cm**.
5	5cm	The length of the diameter of a circle is double the length of the radius. Therefore, the length of the radius is 10cm ÷ 2 = **5cm**.
6	4	A rhombus is a quadrilateral therefore it has **4** sides, which are all equal in length.
7	nonagon	A nine-sided shape is called a **nonagon**.
8	240m	100m + 100m + 20m + 20m = **240m**
9	28m	Side length: $\sqrt{49m^2} = 7m$ Therefore, the perimeter is 7m × 4 = **28m**.
10	24cm^2	Area of square: 8cm × 8cm = 64cm^2 Area of rectangle: 10cm × 4cm = 40cm^2 Therefore, the difference is 64cm^2 – 40cm^2 = **24cm^2**.
11	88mm^2	Number of squares in rectangle: 8 Therefore, the area is 8 × 11mm^2 = **88mm^2**.
12	12cm^2	Area of triangle: $^1/_2$ × base × perpendicular height $^1/_2$ × 6cm × 4cm = **12cm^2**
13	4	A square has **4** lines of symmetry.
14	6	A regular hexagon has an order of rotational symmetry of **6**.
15	4	Shape **4** has an incorrect line of symmetry.

Question	Answer	Explanation
1	21	The triangle has 3 sides, the octagon 8 sides, the hexagon 6 sides and the rectangle 4 sides. The total number of sides in the 4 shapes is 3 + 8 + 6 + 4 = **21**.
2	trapezium	The shape is a **trapezium**.
3	5	Of the seven terms, **5** are associated with circles. A sector, arc, diameter, circumference and semicircle are all names of parts of a circle. A corner and a polygon have nothing to do with circles.
4	12.5cm	Side length of square: 50 ÷ 2 = 25cm The diameter of the circle equals the length of one side of the square. As the radius = diameter ÷ 2, 25cm ÷ 2 = **12.5cm**.
5	60%	A polygon is a shape with three or more straight sides. Therefore, all five shapes are polygons. Of the five shapes, the square, regular octagon and the rectangle are the only shapes with at least one pair of perpendicular sides. As a percentage this is $^3/_5 \times 100$ = **60%**.
6	1	A regular quadrilateral is a shape with 4 equal straight sides and 4 equal angles. Of the five shapes, the square is the only regular quadrilateral.
7	hexagon	The interior angles in a **hexagon** sum to 720°.
8	2.1km	16800m ÷ 8 = 2100m = **2.1km**
9	$4a$	The perimeter of the square is $a + a + a + a$ = **$4a$**.
10	17.77cm	5.28cm + 6.47cm + 6.02cm = **17.77cm**
11	135cm^2	The number of full squares which the shape covers is 7. The number of half squares that the shape covers is 6, which makes 3 further full squares. Therefore, the shape covers 7 + 3 = 10 full squares in total. As the area of one square is 13.5cm^2, the area of 10 squares is 13.5cm^2 × 10 = **135cm^2**.
12	40mm	Area of rectangle = length × width 36cm^2 = 9cm x Y Y = 36cm^2 ÷ 9cm = 4cm = **40mm**
13	6	**6** of the 7 letters have at least one line of symmetry. The only one that does not is the letter Q.
14	8	The full shape is a regular octagon, which has order of rotational symmetry of **8**.
15	11	One square has 4 lines of symmetry, so two squares have 8 lines of symmetry. A kite has 1 line of symmetry. A rectangle has 2 lines of symmetry. A parallelogram has no lines of symmetry. Therefore, in total the shapes have 8 + 1 + 2 = **11** lines of symmetry.

Chapter 11: 2D Shapes, Perimeter, Area and Symmetry - Advanced

Question	Answer	Explanation
1	3,000cm	3m + 6m + 2m + 3m + 6m + 4m + 2m + 4m = 30m = **3000cm**
2	no	If the longest side of a rectangle is 18.5cm, then the smallest side must be less than 18.5cm. The maximum area must therefore be smaller than 18.5cm × 18.5cm = 342.25cm^2.
3	30cm	Diameter of smaller circle: $^3/_7$ × 1.4m = 0.6m Therefore, the radius of the smaller circle is 0.6m ÷ 2 = 0.3m = **30cm**.
4	25%	Of the 8 letters, 2 letters (H and X) have both line symmetry and rotational symmetry. $^2/_8$ × 100 = **25%**
5	84cm^2	Length of longest side: 52cm – (18cm + 5cm + 5cm) = 52cm – 28cm = 24cm Area of trapezium = $^1/_2$ × h × (a + b) (where a and b are the parallel sides and h is the perpendicular height) Therefore, the area is $^1/_2$ × 4cm × (18cm + 24cm) = $^1/_2$ × 4cm × 42cm = **84cm^2**.
6	kite	A **kite** is the object in question.
7	7	4 of the 7 shapes have parallel sides. 1 + 2 + 1 + 3 = **7**
8	100m^2	Area of larger rectangle: 12m × 6m = 72m^2 Area of smaller rectangle: 8m × 3m = 24m^2 Therefore, the area of the whole shape is 72m^2 + 24m^2 = 96m^2. 96m^2 rounded to the nearest 10m^2 is **100m^2**.
9	3(b + c)	The perimeter is given by the expression $b + b + b + c + c + c = 3b + 3c = $ **3(b + c)**.
10	4	The shape has **4** lines of symmetry in total.
11	20.4cm	Diameter of circle: 17mm × 2 = 34mm The diameter of one circle, 34mm, is also the width of the rectangle and the diameter of both circles, 34mm × 2 = 68mm, is the length of the rectangle. Therefore, the perimeter is (34mm × 2) + (68mm × 2) = 68mm + 136mm = 204mm = **20.4cm**.
12	B and E	**B** is false because the parallelogram is also irregular. **E** is false as only two of the four shapes are quadrilaterals.
13	11.16m^2	Area of rectangle: 4m × 6m = 24m^2 Area of triangle: $^1/_2$ × 4.5m × 8m = 18m^2 Area of square: 5.4m × 5.4m = 29.16m^2 Therefore, the difference between the largest area and the smallest area is 29.16m^2 – 18m^2 = **11.16m^2**.
14	7	Side length of square: 16cm ÷ 4 = 4cm Area of square: 4cm × 4cm = 16cm^2 Therefore, the number of whole squares that could be cut from the material is 113.8cm^2 ÷ 16cm^2 = 7.1125 → **7** whole squares.
15	16.5cm	Area of triangle: $^1/_2$ × base × perpendicular height Therefore, its height is 24.75cm^2 ÷ (3cm × $^1/_2$) = 24.75cm^2 ÷ 1.5cm = **16.5cm**.

Chapter 12: 3D Shapes and Volume - Beginner

Question	Answer	Explanation
1	cylinder	This 3D shape is called a **cylinder**.
2	18	The top and the base each have 6 edges and there are 6 edges connecting the ends. Therefore, the total number of edges is 6 + 6 + 6 = **18**.
3	square-based pyramid	This 3D shape is called a **square-based pyramid**.
4	8	A cuboid has **8** vertices.
5	7	A pentagonal prism has **7** faces.
6	triangular prism	When folded up, the net forms a **triangular prism**.
7	closed	When folded up, the net forms a **closed** cube.
8	tetrahedron	When folded up, the net forms a **tetrahedron** or triangular pyramid.
9	120m^3	8m × 3m × 5m = **120m^3**
10	3cm	$\sqrt[3]{27cm^3}$ = **3cm**
11	264cm^3	11cm × 6cm × 4cm = **264cm^3**
12	60cm^3	Number of cubes: 5 × 3 × 2 = 30 Therefore, the volume is 2cm^3 × 30 = **60cm^3**.
13	8	64cm^3 ÷ 8cm^3 = **8**
14	B	Volume of cuboid A: 5cm × 10cm × 8cm = 400cm^3 Volume of cuboid B: 6cm × 11cm × 6cm = 396cm^3 Cuboid **B** has the smaller volume.
15	70m^3	Volume of cube B: 40m^3 × $^3/_4$ = 30m^3 Therefore, the combined volume is 40m^3 + 30m^3 = **70m^3**.

Question	Answer	Explanation
1	3	A cube has **3** pairs of parallel faces.
2	4	A cuboid has 12 edges and a square-based pyramid has 8 edges. Therefore, the difference is 12 − 8 = **4**.
3	15	The tetrahedron has 4 faces, the cylinder 3 faces and the octahedron 8 faces. Therefore, the total number of faces is 4 + 3 + 8 = **15**.
4	hexagonal prism	A triangular prism has 6 vertices. The shape with twice this number of vertices (which is 2 × 6 = 12) is a **hexagonal prism**.
5	3	Number of spheres: 26 ÷ 2 = 13 Therefore, the number of boxes that can be filled is 13 ÷ 4 = 3.25 → **3** full boxes.
6	9cm	The smallest faces have been shaded in grey. Therefore, the perimeter is (2.1cm × 2) + (2.4cm × 2) = 4.2cm + 4.8cm = **9cm**.
7	6	A regular octagonal prism consists of 8 identical rectangles and 2 identical octagons for its faces. Therefore, Alina requires **6** more identical rectangles.
8	2m	Volume of cuboid = length × height × breadth Therefore the breadth is $120m^3 \div (6m \times 10m) = 120m^3 \div 60m^2 = $ **2m**.
9	180m^3	12m × 5m × 300cm = 12m × 5m × 3m = **180m^3**
10	125cm^3	If the area of a cube is 25cm^2, the side length must be √25cm = 5cm. Therefore, the volume is 5cm × 5cm × 5cm = **125cm^3**.
11	80cm^3	Volume of wedge = $\frac{1}{2}$ × length × height × breadth $\frac{1}{2}$ × 8cm × 4cm × 5cm = **80cm^3**
12	D	Face **D** is parallel to the base of the cube when it is folded up.
13	250cm^3	The cuboid consists of 20 cubes and each cube has a volume of 12.5cm^3. Therefore, the volume is 20 × 12.5cm^2 = **250cm^3**.
14	850cm^3	Volume of cylinder = area of circular base × height 50cm^2 × 17cm = **850cm^3**
15	140cm^3	IVcm = 4cm, VIIcm = 7cm, Vcm = 5cm Therefore, the volume is 4cm × 7cm × 5cm = **140cm^3**.

Question	Answer	Explanation
1	39	3 cubes: 3 × 6 = 18 faces 2 hexagonal prisms: 2 × 8 = 16 faces 1 triangular prism: 5 faces Therefore, the total number of faces is 18 + 16 + 5 = **39**.
2	2	A regular octagonal prism is comprised of 8 rectangles and 2 octagons. Each rectangle has 2 pairs of parallel edges and each octagon has 4 pairs of parallel edges. Therefore, the only faces with 3 or more pairs of parallel edges are the **2** octagons.
3	39	The shapes have the following number of vertices; cube (8), triangular prism (6), tetrahedron (4), pentagonal prism (10), square-based pyramid (5) and triangular wedge (6). Therefore, the total number of vertices is 8 + 6 + 4 + 10 + 5 + 6 = **39**.
4	104.1m	Each cone measures 30cm across. Therefore, the minimum length of the road would occur when the cones are all in a line next to each other, which would measure 30cm × 347 = 10410cm = **104.1m**.
5	2	A cuboid has 6 faces (triangular number), a triangular prism has 5 (prime number), a tetrahedron has 4, a pentagonal prism has 7 (prime number), a square-based pyramid has 5 (prime number) and an octahedron has 8. Only **two** of the six shapes do not have a prime or triangular number of faces.
6	13.25cm^3	16 cubes make up the cuboid. Therefore, each cube has a volume of 212cm^3 ÷ 16 = **13.25cm^3**.
7	220.5cm^3	3.5cm × 9cm × 70mm = 3.5cm × 9cm × 7cm = **220.5cm^3**
8	36	Each marble is 2cm in diameter so you could have 8 ÷ 2 = 4 marbles in length, 6 ÷ 2 = 3 marbles in height and 6 ÷ 2 = 3 marbles in breadth. Therefore, the number of marbles that would fit is 4 × 3 × 3 = **36**.
9	2,940cm^3	The shape can be split into two cuboids. Volume of shorter cuboid: 18cm × 10cm × 5cm = 900cm^3 Volume of longer cuboid: (160mm + 18cm) × 12cm × 5cm = (16cm + 18cm) × 12cm × 5cm = 34cm × 12cm × 5cm = 2040cm^3 Therefore, the volume of the whole shape is 900cm^3 + 2040cm^3 = **2940cm^3**.
10	24cm	If the volume of a cube is 216cm^2, the side length must be $^3\sqrt{216}$cm = 6cm. Therefore, the perimeter is 6cm × 4 = **24cm**.
11	34.56cm^3	32 cubes make up the cuboid. Each cube has a volume of 1.08cm^3. Therefore, the volume of the cuboid is 32 × 1.08cm^3 = **34.56cm^3**.
12	181.7cm^3	(25.8cm^3 × 4) + (15.7cm^3 × 5) = 103.2cm^3 + 78.5cm^3 = **181.7cm^3**
13	7cm	Volume of cylinder: area of circular base × height Height: 2000cm^3 ÷ 100cm^2 = 20cm Therefore, the depth is 20cm – 13cm = **7cm**.
14	60mm	Volume of cuboid = length × height × breadth Therefore, the breadth is 210cm^3 ÷ (5cm × 7cm) = 210cm^3 ÷ 35cm^2 = 6cm = **60mm**.
15	336cm^3	Breadth: 3.5 × 8cm = 28cm Height: $^3/_{16}$ × 8cm = 1.5cm Therefore, the volume is 8cm × 28cm × 1.5cm = **336cm^3**.

Chapter 13: Probability - Beginner

Question	Answer	Explanation
1	impossible	It is **impossible** for February to contain more than 29 days.
2	likely	It is **likely** to rain on at least one day during March in London.
3	even chance	There are only 2 outcomes when tossing a fair coin so there is an **even chance** of the coin landing on either heads or tails.
4	certain	Someone under the age of 21 cannot become prime minister so it is **certain** that they will be over the age of 10.
5	unlikely	It is **unlikely** for a brand new car to break down 2 days in a row.
6	$^1/_3$	The probability of landing on grey is $^2/_6 = ^1/_3$.
7	0.5	There are 3 even and 3 odd numbers on a fair die. Therefore, the probability of the die landing on an even number is $^3/_6 = ^1/_2 = $ **0.5**.
8	$^7/_8$	Only one disc has a 3 on it. Therefore, the probability of selecting a disc without a 3 is $^7/_8$.
9	0.2	One of the five letters is a G, which as a decimal is $^1/_5 = $ **0.2**.
10	100%	It is certain that the day after Monday is Tuesday, so the probability is **100%**.
11	$^1/_{26}$	The probability of selecting one of the two cards is $^2/_{52} = ^1/_{26}$.
12	0	It is impossible to select a green marble as **none** of the marbles in the bag are that colour.
13	$^4/_5$	The probability of selecting a page with a photograph is $^8/_{10} = ^4/_5$.
14	$^2/_3$	On a fair die, there are four numbers greater than 2, which as a fraction is $^4/_6 = ^2/_3$.
15	$^2/_3$	Six of the nine circles are shaded, which as a fraction is $^6/_9 = ^2/_3$.

Question	Answer	Explanation
1	certain	It is **certain** that at least one leap year will occur in the next 8 years as they occur every 4 years.
2	unlikely	It is **unlikely** that the number 6 will not occur at all when rolling a fair dice 12 times.
3	impossible	It is **impossible** that tomorrow is Sunday if today is Friday.
4	even chance	Two of the four months have 31 days (January and December) and the other two have 30 days. Therefore, there is an **even chance** ($^2/_4$) that a month chosen from these at random has 31 days.
5	likely	It is **likely** to select a season at random with the letter n in its name as 3 out of the 4 season names contain an n.
6	$^1/_{20}$	Number of squares: $8 \times 5 = 40$ 2 squares contain the image of a bicycle, which as a fraction is $^2/_{40} = ^1/_{20}$.
7	$^1/_{13}$	There are 26 red cards in a pack of 52 playing cards. Of the 26 red cards there are 2 aces and 2 kings, making a total of 4 aces or kings, which as a fraction of all cards is $^4/_{52} = ^1/_{13}$.
8	0.25	P(both tails) $= ^1/_2 \times ^1/_2 = ^1/_4 =$ **0.25**
9	$^5/_9$	There are 9 students in total with 2 scoring 5 and 3 scoring 8. Therefore, the fraction of students scoring 5 or 8 is $^{(2+3)}/_9 = ^5/_9$.
10	$^2/_7$	2 of the 7 days of the week have 8 letters in their name (Thursday and Saturday), which as a fraction is $^2/_7$.
11	$^5/_6$	Of the 6 faces on the spinner, 5 have numbers on them which are less than or equal to 15. As a fraction this is $^5/_6$.
12	$^1/_3$	2 faces on a dice contain an odd number which is greater than 1 (3 and 5). As a fraction of the 6 faces this is $^2/_6 = ^1/_3$.
13	$^5/_9$	The bag consists of $15 + 12 = 27$ balls in total. 15 of these balls are not purple, which as a fraction of all balls is $^{15}/_{27} = ^5/_9$.
14	15	$18 \times ^5/_6 =$ **15**
15	25%	2 of the 8 subjects begin with the letter m (maths and music), which as a percentage is $^2/_8 \times 100 = ^1/_4 \times 100 =$ **25%**.

Question	Answer	Explanation
1	$^1/_2$	The probability of obtaining exactly one head and one tail from tossing two coins is either obtaining a head and a tail or a tail and a head. Therefore, the probability is (P(heads) × P(tails)) + (P(tails) × P(heads)) = ($^1/_2 × ^1/_2$) + ($^1/_2 × ^1/_2$) = $^1/_4 + ^1/_4$ = $^1/_2$.
2	$^7/_{24}$	After removing the 4 cards, there are 48 left, of which 13 – 2 = 11 are diamonds. There are four queens in a pack and none have been removed, but one of the queens is also a diamond, so there are three further queens to add to the 11 diamonds. Therefore, P(diamond or queen) = $^{(11+3)}/_{48}$ = $^{14}/_{48}$ = $^7/_{24}$.
3	$^1/_6$	The number of combinations that make a total of 7 when rolling two dice are 1 & 6, 2 & 5, 3 & 4, 4 & 3, 5 & 2 and 6 & 1, so the total of 7 can be obtained 6 ways. There are 36 combinations in total, so P(total of 7) = $^6/_{36}$ = $^1/_6$.
4	75%	There are 8 sections on the spinner, 3 are grey and 3 are white. Therefore, the probability is $^{(3+3)}/_8$ = $^6/_8$ = $^3/_4$ = **75%**.
5	$^7/_{11}$	Number of coins in purse: 3 + 5 + 8 + 6 = 22 Number of coins worth at least 50 pence: 8 + 6 = 14 Therefore, the probability is $^{14}/_{22}$ = $^7/_{11}$.
6	38	P(less than 3) = P(1 or 2) = $^2/_6 × 114$ = $^1/_3 × 114$ = **38**
7	$^1/_3$	Three of the nine discs are larger than 5 but no larger than 12 (6, 7 and 12), which as a fraction is $^3/_9$ = $^1/_3$.
8	$^1/_{84}$	P(C) = $^2/_8$ = $^1/_4$, P(A) = $^2/_7$, P(P) = $^1/_6$ Therefore, P(CAP) = $^1/_4 × ^2/_7 × ^1/_6$ = $^2/_{168}$ = $^1/_{84}$.
9	$^{27}/_{52}$	P(loss) = 1 – ($^3/_{13} + ^1/_4$) = 1 – ($^{12}/_{52} + ^{13}/_{52}$) = 1 – $^{25}/_{52}$ = $^{27}/_{52}$
10	24%	Set 1: P(shaded) = $^{15}/_{25}$ = $^3/_5$ Set 2: P(shaded) = $^{10}/_{25}$ = $^2/_5$ Therefore, the probability that both are shaded is $^3/_5 × ^2/_5$ = $^6/_{25}$ = **24%**.
11	14	P(less than two errors) = 6% + 29% = 35% Therefore, the number of books is 40 × 35% = 40 × 0.35 = **14**.
12	39	$^3/_8 × 104$ = **39**
13	E	P(ace of hearts) = $^1/_{52}$ is not equal to P(black ace) = $^1/_{26}$.
14	impossible	A double headed coin can only ever land heads up.
15	$^1/_3$	P(head) = $^1/_2$ P(not 1 or 6) = $^4/_6$ = $^2/_3$ Therefore, the probability is $^1/_2 × ^2/_3$ = $^2/_6$ = $^1/_3$.

Question	Answer	Explanation
1	D	Point **D** is at coordinates (2, 3).
2	(0, 3)	x-coordinate: (0 + 0) ÷ 2 = 0 y-coordinate: (1 + 5) ÷ 2 = 6 ÷ 2 = 3 Therefore, the coordinates of the midpoint are **(0, 3)**.
3	(8, 6)	Point Q is at coordinates **(8, 6)**.
4	right-angled	The coordinates (0, 0), (3, 0) and (0, 4) form a **right-angled** triangle.
5	(3, 1)	The ship is at coordinates **(3, 1)**.
6	(1, 2) and (4, 5)	To form a trapezium, a straight line must be drawn between the coordinates **(1, 2)** and **(4, 5)**.
7	(0, 5)	Point V at coordinates (5, 0) is rotated 90° anticlockwise about the origin to its new position of **(0, 5)**.
8	(4, 1)	Point A at coordinates (1, 1) is translated 3 units right to its new position of **(4, 1)**.
9	kite	The coordinates (3, 0), (5, 4), (3, 6) and (1, 4) form a **kite**.
10	(1, 3)	Point Q at coordinates (2, 0) is translated three units up, then one unit left to its new position of **(1, 3)**.
11	(4, 4)	The centre point at coordinates (3, 2) is translated two units up, then one unit right to its new position of **(4, 4)**.
12	(4, 2)	Point B at coordinates (0, 2) is reflected in the line x = 2, taking it to point **(4, 2)**.
13	(4, 4)	Point J at coordinates (4, 2) is reflected in the line y = 3, taking it to point **(4, 4)**.
14	(10, 3)	After the two transformations, the new coordinates for point Z are **(10, 3)**.
15	(1, 3)	Point F at coordinates (1, −3) is reflected in the x-axis, taking it to point **(1, 3)**.

Chapter 14: Coordinates and Transformations - Intermediate

Question	Answer	Explanation
1	Q	Point **Q** is at coordinates (–4, 4).
2	**(8, y)**	A horizontal straight line will have the same y-coordinates throughout. The midpoint x-coordinate will be (5 + 11) ÷ 2 = 16 ÷ 2 = 8. Therefore, the midpoint coordinates are **(8, y)**.
3	**(–3, 3)**	Point **(–3, 3)** lies vertically to the point (–3, 9) as they share the same x-coordinate.
4	**(–5, –2)**	The length of one side of the square is 5 + 1 = 6 units. The last corner coordinates are therefore (1 – 6, 4 – 6) = **(–5, –2)**.
5	**(2, –3)**	The coffee shop is at coordinates **(2, –3)**.
6	**(6, 2)**	Point C is at coordinates **(6, 2)**.
7	**(–4, 2)**	The coordinates of the last corner of the parallelogram are **(–4, 2)**.
8	**(–1, –2)**	Point G at coordinates (1, 2) is rotated 180° clockwise about the point (0, 0), taking point G to coordinates **(–1, –2)**.
9	S	The coordinates of point T, when translated 30 units left, change from (10, –40) to (–20, –40). These are the same coordinates as point **S**.
10	**(33, –7)**	Point V is at coordinates (30, –12 + 5) = (30, –7). It is translated 3 units right, which takes it to coordinates (30 + 3, –7) = **(33, –7)**.
11	A	Diagram **A** shows the rectangle rotated 45° clockwise about its centre.
12	**(1, 4)**	Point c is at coordinates (4, 4). It is reflected in the line x = 2.5, which takes point c to coordinates **(1, 4)**.
13	L5	Point Q must be reflected in line **L5** to move it to point P.
14	horizontal line that joins the coordinates (0, 2) and (5, 2)	The line y = 2 is made up of points which all share the same y-coordinate of 2. This results in a horizontal line that intercepts the y-axis at coordinates (0, 2).
15	**(1, 1)**	Point C is at coordinates (4, 2). Shape S is rotated clockwise through 90° about the point (2, 3), taking point C to coordinates **(1, 1)**.

Question	Answer	Explanation
1	(8.5, −18)	In an isosceles triangle the x-coordinate of the third corner will occur halfway between the x-coordinates of the other two corners, which is (15 + 2) ÷ 2 = 17 ÷ 2 = 8.5. Therefore, the coordinates of the third corner are **(8.5, −18)**.
2	(40, 40)	Point R at coordinates (−40, 10) is rotated 270° anticlockwise about point (0, 0) to its new position of (10, 40). Point P at coordinates **(40, 40)** is directly east of this.
3	(−9.5, 7)	Point Z is translated 4 units left from (−5.5, −7) to (−9.5, −7). It is then reflected in the x-axis, taking it to coordinates **(−9.5, 7)**.
4	(−2, 4)	After the two transformations, the only point where the two shapes touch is at **(−2, 4)**.
5	4	A circle has centre coordinates (2, 0). Its diameter is 4 units, which means the smallest x-coordinate on its circumference is 0 and the largest x-coordinate is **4**.
6	(2.5, 3) and (2.5, −1)	The length of one side of the square is 4.5 − 0.5 = 4 units. The x-coordinate of the centre of the square must occur halfway between the two end points, which is (4.5 + 0.5) ÷ 2 = 2.5. The y-coordinate of the centre of the square is 4 ÷ 2 = 2 units above or below 1, which is 3 or −1. Therefore, the possible coordinates are **(2.5, 3)** and **(2.5, −1)**.
7	270°	The point (1, 1) must be rotated **270°** clockwise about the origin to become (−1, 1).
8	(2, 5)	Point C at coordinates (−2, 5) is rotated 270° anticlockwise about point (0, 3) to its new position of **(2, 5)**.
9	315°	After moving in a straight line from point (4, 4) to (1, 1), Prasha only needs to rotate 45° clockwise before moving in another straight line to point (−5, 1). However, she turns through a reflex angle so the size of the angle she turns through is 360° − 45° = **315°**.
10	(−4, 1)	Point N at coordinates (2, −1) is rotated 180° clockwise about point (−1, 0), taking point N to coordinates **(−4, 1)**.
11	(0, 1)	The point that lies exactly halfway between point L (−2, 3) and point N (2, −1) is **(0, 1)**, therefore making it the midpoint.
12	$\begin{pmatrix} 3 \\ 4 \end{pmatrix}$	Point M is translated 3 units right and then 4 units up. Therefore, the translation is $\begin{pmatrix} 3 \\ 4 \end{pmatrix}$.
13	draw point K at (−2, −3)	The coordinates of point L when reflected in the x-axis are **(−2, −3)**.
14	(−3, −3)	After the two transformations, the new coordinates for point M are **(−3, −3)**.
15	(−1, 2)	After the two transformations, the new coordinates for point N are **(−1, 2)**.